WHOLE-BODY INTIMACY

Whole-Body Intimacy allows couples and their therapists to deepen their understanding of the essential components of intimate relationships and create meaningful sexual connection.

This book brings somatic sex therapy into the interpersonal realm by applying Walker's Somatic-Concentric Sex Therapy model to the sexual intimacy of couples and those in intimate relationships. Offering a whole-body somatic approach to intimacy, this book embeds cognitive and emotional components within body-to-body sexuality and can be modulated to help individuals navigate common sexual difficulties, such as desire difference or other sexual challenges, as the body changes and encounters medical or health events across the lifespan. The chapters provide full coverage on assumptions about intimacy, desire difference, the sexual response cycle, attachment, bodyful practices, as well as a guide to embodied consent. With experiential guides and reflective questions to help the readers apply the material directly to their relationship, this book takes readers on a whole-person, three-dimensional journey that integrates all aspects of the social-sexual self within an interpersonal connection. Readers will increase knowledge of desires, boundaries, relational patterns, and growth edges in intimate relationships.

This book is an essential resource for therapists, clients of sex therapy, relational therapy, couples counseling, and premarital counseling, as well as those looking to deepen their understanding of intimate relationships.

Melissa Walker, LPC, CST, R-DMT, is Licensed Professional Counselor, American Association for Sex Educators, Counselors, and Therapists (AASECT) Certified Sex Therapist, and Dance/Movement Therapist, and the director of Embodied Relationships Counseling and Training Center in Colorado. Her first book, *Whole-Body Sex*, received the 2023 AASECT General Audience Book Award.

"With the publishing of *Whole-Body Intimacy*, Melissa Walker has singlehandedly extended and deepened our understanding of sexuality, relationship, and embodiment in both conceptual and practical ways. Taking the idea of whole body to heart, she deftly guides us through the complexities of pleasure, intimacy, and sexuality with a grace and wisdom that feel both sensible and transformational. She introduces us to many different ideas and practices, such as Moving at the Pace of Connection, Sex as Self-Defined, Intimacy as both freestanding (as in sexual acts) and embedded (as in moment-by-moment sensations, feelings, glances), the Whole Person Sexual Response Cycle, Everyday Eroticism, Erotic Mapping, and Pleasure Heals the Body. Both accessible and comprehensive, she casts a clear eye on thorny topics such as consent, health challenges, desire differences, aging, and infidelity with grace and wisdom, and then gives us meaningful and powerful practices to investigate these areas in our own bodies and relationships. Whoever you are, whatever your sexual nature at this point in your life, this book is written for YOU."

Christine Caldwell, *PhD, LPC, BC-DMT, Professor Emeritus, Naropa University, Somatic Counseling Psychology, author*

"With clarity and compassion, Melissa Walker gently guides the reader into whole-body listening, inviting attuned awareness of the body's rhythms, histories, and signals within intimacy. *Whole-Body Intimacy* offers an integrative framework that honors personal process and supports honest, bodyful partnerships rooted in embodied consent. A nourishing contribution for readers and clinicians alike seeking intimacy beyond assumption and toward embodied understanding."

Christina Devereaux, *PhD, LMHC, LPC, LCAT, BC-DMT, NCC, board-certified dance/movement therapist, international trainer, educator, author*

"Melissa writes with a compassion and precision that made the book feel immediately relevant, offering an accessible guide for softening nervous-system overwhelm and reclaiming intimacy through embodied consent. *Whole-Body Intimacy* offers the language, practices, and somatic maps many of us were never taught, illuminating the developmental realities of pregnancy, menopause, andropause, non-sexual seasons, and perimenopausal and post-menopausal transitions with a clarity that feels both validating and liberating. Her approach invites us to rediscover and re-create our arousal anatomy, cultivate everyday pleasure, and return to the erotic gateways that make us feel vividly alive."

Tomoyo Kawano, *PhD, BC-DMT, LCAT, NCC, Associate Professor and Director, MA in Dance/Movement Therapy at Antioch University*

"*Whole-Body Intimacy* is an essential glimpse into the vast psychological and physiological principles of intimacy. Melissa Walker leads readers into territory that is rarely addressed but entirely necessary, outlining constructs that cover skills-based, somatic paths toward fulfilling relationships. This book is an invaluable resource for creating an attuned and embodied relational life."

Holly Richmond, *PhD, author of* Reclaiming Pleasure: A Sex-Positive Guide for Moving Past Sexual Trauma and Living a Passionate Life

WHOLE-BODY INTIMACY

A Pathway to Embodied Connection Across the Lifespan

Melissa Walker

Routledge
Taylor & Francis Group
NEW YORK AND LONDON

Designed cover image: Getty Images

First published 2027
by Routledge
605 Third Avenue, New York, NY 10158

and by Routledge
4 Park Square, Milton Park, Abingdon, Oxon, OX14 4RN

Routledge is an imprint of the Taylor & Francis Group, an informa business

ISBN: 978-1-032-83364-4 (hbk)
ISBN: 978-1-032-83251-7 (pbk)
ISBN: 978-1-003-50898-4 (ebk)

DOI: 10.4324/9781003508984

Typeset in Minion
by Apex CoVantage, LLC

In deep gratitude to my partner and family.
In honor of my clients and students.

CONTENTS

AUTHOR'S NOTE

My first book, *Whole-Body Sex,* focused on the individual and their relationship with their own embodied sexuality. On the day of my virtual book release party in January of 2021, in the throes of the COVID pandemic, I was diagnosed with early-stage breast cancer. In the unknown terror of those first moments, I could feel the underworld journey beginning within, and I made a commitment to myself that I would stay deeply connected with my body through the entire healing process.

My outer life stopped, and I turned inward to focus on my recovery and spend time with my beloved family. The embodiment principles and bodyful practices that I wrote in *Whole-Body Sex* were my moment-to-moment guide, reminding me to move at the pace of my body and to cultivate pleasure even in the midst of immense pain and uncertainty. As a result of my dedication to my body, the support of my family and friends, and the talent of my surgeons, my healing has extended far beyond my physical body into all aspects of my life.

The book that you hold in your hands, *Whole-Body Intimacy,* became a natural extension of my journey as my partner and I navigated the healing of my body together. We applied the *Whole-Body Sex* principles to our relationship and daily interactions. We created shared intimacy values that honored our changing roles and my changing body. We communicated clearly and with genuine feeling, validating each other as we experienced the full range of emotions, sometimes aligned and sometimes not. We learned more about our unique relationship styles, how we complimented each other well, and how we transitioned into attunement. Sometimes, I would sit at the dinner table with tears—my body would just need to cry—and my partner would hold my hand, knowing that this wave of emotion would transform into what was next: relief, laughter, and gratitude. Our connection strengthened, and our journey became deeply meaningful. Working together, we fueled our evolution.

I discovered many important things on this journey. One of the most remarkable is that pleasure—connective, consensual, intentional pleasure—is not frivolous. In fact, pleasure *heals*. The pleasure in my daily walk around the park. The pleasure in sitting by my fire as the tension in my back softened and opened. The pleasure in my partner's touch and embracing gaze.

As I applied this learning to my work as a couples therapist, I realized that this is true for others as well. My client's relationships have deepened. Their awareness and expressiveness have volumized.

This book presents the modified knowledge and bodyful practices of *Whole-Body Sex* so that you too can learn how they apply to your intimate connection and how to practice together. It is an invitation and guide to cultivate embodied pleasure and connection in your relationship, not just to be happier, but to get the most out of life, no matter what challenges you face.

A philosopher once said that the obstacle becomes the way. Whether you and your partner experience a desire difference or are managing a challenging health condition, obstacles are a part of being a sexual being in a relationship. This book is about learning to move with your body, to press into what may feel like an obstacle but is actually a tender part of you waiting for contact and understanding in order to transform into what is next.

My hope is that you find deep meaningfulness in the journey that is your intimate relationship so that you and your partner can grow together and alongside each other to be more of who you are.

INTRODUCTION

A Vision of Bodyful Intimacy

I hear the door chime as Kyle and Brittany enter my office for their first appointment. I welcome them inside, seating them across from me on a modern blue couch with large ochre pillows, light filling the room from the large picture windows. They sit on either side of the couch, Brittany slightly angled toward Kyle as he sits straight, facing me. The space between them speaks volumes, and I'm here to get to the bottom of the dynamic that they are already demonstrating as they settle onto my couch.

I begin our session with some of my typical questions. What does sex and intimacy mean to you? Why is it important, and how does it impact you as an individual and the roles that you hold in life? What does sex mean for you based on your gender, race, socioeconomic class, body ability, and so on?

Over the last 15 years, I have worked with hundreds of couples like Kyle and Brittany who arrive in my office with intimacy challenges of all kinds, from desire differences to medical factors impacting their sex life, to infidelity, to hoping to rediscover their sexual connection after having kids or kids moving out of the home.

In my work, I've found that the most insightful shifts come from identifying how the body created protective armor against the uncomfortable messages and experiences involving the body and sexuality while discovering the places and activities that were safe enough for sexuality to flow and express creatively. These are the lines of questions that allow for validation, compassion, and, ultimately, revelation. For Brittany, this looked like exploring how her relationship to intimacy had begun to change due to perimenopause, which had triggered old negative messages from her teenage years about her body and female desire more broadly. In exploring her history and how it impacted her body in the current time, we found that she held a lot of

DOI: 10.4324/9781003508984-1

muscle tension in her pelvis and in her chest, which made sex unpleasant and difficult to communicate that she wanted something different. Meanwhile, though she had trouble expressing herself in the intimate realm, she found confidence and the easeful pleasure of movement on her yoga mat several times a week. For Kyle, we found that he had been bullied as a young boy, and so his body had shrunk his expression, making his emotional state difficult for Brittany to read and challenging to connect with him in an intimate way. Though he had trouble expressing intimate emotions with his partner, Kyle found fuller expression through singing in a local choir. To embrace oneself while in a state of discomfort or confusion—with "that makes sense that you protected yourself that way" and "how wonderful that your sexuality still found a safe enough place to express"—this was the key to unlock a new phase for Kyle and Brittany.

The culture that you grow up in weaves itself into the fabric of your body and mind. It impacts what you believe and how your body organizes around sex. It informs your breath quality, movement, expression or suppression of desire, whether or not you can receive pleasure, whether you can feel relaxed and excited, as well as your tendency to emphasize one person's pleasure, comfort, and desire over the other's. Every time I explore with my clients what they've learned, we uncover the places where being in their body is uncomfortable and expressing sexuality is accompanied by the shoulds and should-nots. This is the place where fully inhabiting the body—awake and in the present moment—is incredibly difficult. This is also often the root of a couple's challenging dynamic since these old discomforts get activated in the present moment of intimate interactions. This is the root that we apply a somatic creative process to in order to activate deep understanding and transformation.

Once I learn the origins of Kyle and Brittany's foundation, we turn to visioning with the golden ticket question—*what do you want sex and intimacy to mean to you?* And *what role do you want it to play in your relationship?*

This is the question that helps couples develop *shared intimacy values* and underscores the habits and practices that guide them to enact these shared values in their day-to-day life. Working as a team to realize and put into practice this deeper purpose allows my clients to inhabit more of themselves, more of their whole body, within the magical space of their intimate connection.

For Kyle and Brittany, they developed shared values of supporting each other in their expressive activities and investing in the practice of transparent and embodied communication as they learned about their intimate dynamic. Through these values, they felt embraced in their individuality, which allowed them to feel inner motivation to share themselves with each other. They began to tell each other their challenging thoughts and feelings about what they did and did not desire in their sexual intimacy. Because they both felt welcomed and valued, they valued the learning process, and a deep closeness developed between them.

At their best, intimate relationships have the potential to bring deep meaning to our lives, elevating the best of times and supporting us when things get difficult. Your intimate partner is the one who brings out your best qualities and challenges you to grow the edges of your potential, while also bolstering their own personal growth journey. Adventures become a shared journey as you traverse important life thresholds. Together, you can be an ally to each other's ever-evolving sexuality as you mature and deepen your capacity to be enlivened through the movement of sexual energy. We are fundamentally wired to be in relationships. Our brain, immune system, and sense of meaning in life depend on it to thrive. This wiring can be leveraged to heal prior wounding in a relationship and establish a deeply satisfying connection with your intimate partner.

The most important thing that I can give my clients is a *sense of purpose* related to their sexuality. This is way beyond the basic functional sexual concerns. A sense of purpose comes from the discovery of how self-defined and relationally relevant (as opposed to socially defined) sexuality can be a life-giving force, supportive of growth, connection, and the deep meaningfulness of a journey worth walking.

Learning Through Relationship

All intimate relationships contain important information for you—pebbles along your journey that coalesce into a path—even though, at times, you may not see the learning value. It's easy to take intimate relationships for granted because we get into the automatic flow of survival while managing the myriad of day-to-day tasks—until a challenge is so great, we are forced to pause and pay attention. It's then people say, "maybe we're just not right for each other," or "we've grown apart," or "we must not be sexually compatible anymore."

Sometimes, this is indeed true. Some relationships are *learning* relationships, characterized by old, ineffective, and sometimes painful relationship habits that are being repeated. This offers the opportunity to learn about the dynamic and figure out how to respond differently, to set boundaries, advocate for yourself, or regulate difficult emotions more quickly. The old habits and patterns are from your early life—your family, early caregivers, and other impactful social environments. When a partner presses these red buttons that were formed, originally, from your relational attachment with a parent, stepparent, or sibling, you get the opportunity to approach it with your adult brain. Now you have a chance to learn about the dynamic, where it comes from, find some understanding, and begin to apply the new learning. In learning relationships, you or your intimate partner are often still entrenched in the old habits and are having trouble making space and grace for each other's humanness.

It's at this juncture that I feel like people don't give themselves or their partners enough credit. You've had so many years of the old way of relating, and, honestly, where would you have learned that people have different styles of communicating, processing information, or experiencing and expressing sexual desire? Unless you decided to research self-help or specialize in psychology, how would you know how trauma affects the nervous system or arousal anatomy? Many of the challenges that couples face are greatly improved with some of this knowledge and a safe enough space to practice these relationship skills.

Yet, sometimes, too much hurt has happened to mend the connection, and a breakthrough is necessary—one or both of you want something different. This is when breakups or affair events often begin.

Other times, relationships are *learning and growing* relationships. Sure, your dynamic has a dash of old patterns, but you also have just enough skill, personal growth, and willingness to learn *together*. You're ready to grow your connective rhythms toward a new, more skillful fork in the road and therefore begin to evolve into more fully embodied intimate partners. In learning and growing relationships, partners know that they missed out on important skills to engage in skillful emotional and intimate relating, and they are ready to put in the work to refine them. Learning and growing relationships are about *evolution*. To be clear, learning relationships can transition into learning and growing or evolutionary relationships when you are up for the challenge.

Intimate relationships are as humbling as they are empowering. They require that you slow down in important moments to identify assumptions and judgments, to be willing to be wrong or share the hard things to say, and to be willing to hear a partner's disappointment or hurt even when you didn't intend to hurt their feelings. There is, after all, an important difference between intention and impact. Intimacy also requires a willingness to *practice receiving* from each other. I often see people focusing on what their partners are or are not doing, meanwhile not being able to receive love, support, sexual interest, and so on when the partner does step in to engage.

This book guides you to approach your connection with your partner from a *learning and growing* perspective, as it offers you the tools to approach your challenges in the present moment with bodyful skills to unwind the ineffective habits from the past.

And since intimate relationships also require some serious contemporary sex education, this book will guide you through understanding and connecting with arousal anatomy to unwind the inaccurate and uninspiring sexual education you have probably received. So very many of us learn about sexuality and partner sex in anxious, fear-inducing, and/or highly sterile medicalized environments. Sex is explained only in a reproductive capacity, and only the bare minimum of reproductive and arousal anatomy (which is often inaccurate) is presented, devoid of the important contextual elements of the nervous system, consensual relationships, gender, and emotions. Even if you visit your medical provider now, it is unlikely that they have an accurate or supportive perspective on sexuality since they, too, receive very little education about sexuality and sexual function, unless they specifically elect to (if you are a medical provider and have sought out sexuality education, well done!). The stories that I hear from my clients are atrocious, and I am very aware that their current understanding of their own sexuality and that of their partner has been built on the rickety foundation of their early sex education. Beginning to question these assumptions and rewire their cognitive and body organization around sex is a big, big adventure—an adventure for you and your partner to set out on together.

This adventure is possible because your nervous systems are literally wired to be in relationship. Our intimate partner allows us to feel parts of ourselves that we cannot access without their presence. Just like in *Castaway*, when Tom Hanks' character drew a face on a volleyball, relationship is core to our beingness and sense of self. We are wired for *call and response*: you laugh and I laugh, and laughing together touches a deep place within, a place of belonging. How we respond to and relate with another through movement, rhythm, touch, tone, and gaze is unique to each relationship, and, as we access these relational parts of ourselves, we are actively creating and recreating the choreography of who we are.

And when we listen closely enough, we can sense our inner growth as we transition into the more fully embodied humans we are meant to be.

Ultimately, this book is an embodied relationship academy of sorts, where you will learn the skills that your academic and social environments didn't teach you. It offers present moment and relational ways to work with the dance of your nervous systems to unravel unsupportive assumptions about your partner's words or behavior—assumptions created from past experiences that take you out of the intimacy of the moment—so that you can embrace the ever-evolving call and response humanness of yourself and your partner.

Getting Into Your Body During Sexual Intimacy

We are often taught ineffective habits and polarizing assumptions that keep us from realizing our relationship potential. We are taught that it is a problem when our partner wants something different sexually than we do or has a different desire expression style (it is not). We are taught that a partner should know what we need or should be a fully skillful lover (unreasonable expectations). We are even taught inaccurate things about arousal anatomy. To this day, many medical textbooks still inaccurately represent the vulvar anatomy (seriously? Yes. At least Wikipedia gets it right.). Additionally, in this current era, we see all kinds of information on social media about sex and intimacy, some of which is great advice and some that is inaccurate or even hurtful to relationships (how do you tell the difference?) We are taught many things that influence how we interpret ourselves and our partner's behavior and influence how we treat each other.

Finally, because we are taught not to talk about sex—or medicalize it, or make it a joke, or use euphemisms—meanwhile being subjected to a firehose of sexual content through the media, many people also have trouble checking out their assumptions so that they can have meaningful conversations about their challenges and strengths. The topic of sex directly impacts your physiology and can create nervous system excitement and/or dysregulation, which prevents a present moment, whole-brain awareness.

In the 16 years that I've been a couple's therapist, including seeing couples in the office and working with groups of couples in retreat or workshop settings, I learned that nervous system dysregulation inevitably happens when the topic of sex comes up. The dysregulation sets the stage for speaking incongruently (feeling and saying different things), making assumptions, not hearing what is actually being communicated, and feeling a lot of discomfort in the form of fear and shame. And *of course,* this is how we respond—our earlier learning environments were often designed to intentionally make sexuality awkward and scary. Having a space to discuss sex and sexuality also sets the stage for discovering resilience and the skills to shift from defensive to receptive, from shadow sexuality into life-affirming embodied sexuality.

So how are we supposed to sift through all the muck to get the intimate connection that we really want? I have one word for you—*Body*. I don't just mean your anatomy, and I don't mean devoid of your intellect. I mean, the way your whole body is organized in the way that makes you *you*. I'm talking about your *somatic architecture*—the organization and expression of the body/mind through the confluence of your life experiences plus your biology. By understanding more about your somatic architecture, you can learn to listen, understand, and communicate from your whole-self so that when you encounter discomfort and an assumption about intimacy, you will skillfully ask yourself and your partner, "Does that actually feel true?" instead of plodding forward as if the assumption *is* true. When intimacy challenges arise, you and your partner will say, "Let's slow down and investigate together." You will learn to be on the same team, with your body and the body of your partner.

You will create your own meaning, together.

Create Your Own Meaning

When Canadian sexology researcher Peggy Kleinplatz and Ménard (2020) asked a diversity of 75 people with an average age of 45.2 years how they define *magnificent sex*, they didn't say things like orgasm, or that their partner could read their mind, or that they used a lot of toys. Instead, research participants emphasized magnificent sex as (1) being completely present and embodied in the moment, (2) moments of feeling fully connected and in synch while being embodied in the moment, (3) a feeling of deep intimacy characterized by mutual respect and trust for their partners, (4) extraordinary communication and deep empathy, (5) being genuine, authentic, and transparent, (6) ability to be vulnerable and surrender "both to the sex itself and to their partners (Kleinplatz 2020, 28)," (7) exploration, interpersonal risk-taking, and fun, and (8) finally, a sense of transcendence and transformation.

Reflecting on the interviews, Kleinplatz said:

> *"Great sex" in no way resembles the media stereotypes. It cannot be found by following pop culture advice for tips, tricks and techniques. On the contrary, in order to find optimal sexual experiences, one must look within. If anything, participants taught us that rather than worrying about setting new bars for magnificent sex unattainably high, they highlighted the need to redefine "sex" per se.*
>
> (Kleinplatz 33)

Somehow (from the dominant culture), many people got the message that sex should be easy and natural with no conversation necessary and, when sex doesn't feel natural, the person with the "difficulty" (often, the one who does not align with the dominant culture definition of sex, which is spontaneous desire, easy building of arousal, followed by orgasm) is willfully rejecting the flow of the moment. Kleinplatz's research shows that great sex is *far more than that.*

When you and a partner begin to intentionally rewire your understanding and practices around sexual intimacy, you will find that it is a vibrant vehicle for personal growth and a source of vitality, when it is relevant to you as a couple and is focused on pleasure and connection. When you and your partner share with each other what is meaningful about your sexual connection, remember to be transparent about what is genuinely felt as you learn more about your personal desire and communication style—not as a flag in the sand, but as a starting point to allow your body the opportunity to be as you are, moment to moment, allowing the unfolding of emotion, desire, and the unwinding of an often-stressed nervous system.

Because we are socialized to be terrible communicators about sex, to define sex and pleasure in narrow ways, and often taught contradictory things about who sex is for or whose pleasure is the most important, it is vital that you slow down and identify what is *actually true* for you. Resist the urge to drop into performative sexuality. Performative sex is when one behaves in ways that they *think* they are supposed to, or according to what they think their partner is supposed to desire, or engage in sex out of obligation as they satisfy the needs of a partner.

This is a *total paradigm shift.*

Now is the moment when you cast performative sex aside and step into your intimate connection with genuine embodiment and transparency. This allows you to begin the rewiring process, unraveling the ideas of sex that you have marinated in through your social, familial, and religious life realms, in order to discover what is relevant. How do you do this? By connecting somatically with yourself and each other, of course, and learning to define sex for yourselves.

Toward a Bodyful Intimacy

Bodyful intimacy is the ebb and flow, the dance, of the consensual intertwining of awake and aware body-to-body connection just as you are. It moves at the pace of connection between you and your partner, slowing down and speeding up, reflecting the tensing and releasing of muscles, and the alternating rhythms of arousal building and dispersing and building again. Bodyful intimacy allows for challenges to arise, then to modulate arousal so you can reconnect with yourself in the present moment and then with a partner, and then to step back into the flow without forcing anything.

To be *bodyful* is to practice placing the whole body, instead of just the mind or fantasy, at the center of the intimacy. This is body-centered mindfulness (Caldwell, 2018): *body*ful instead of *mind*ful. While mindfulness supports a more present and flexible awareness, dislodging attention from intrusive thoughts or feelings so that the mind can witness itself with less judgment and tension, bodyfulness is the practice of witnessing the interrelatedness of mind and body, listening to the physiological signals from the nervous system and refining the ability to attune to the emergent language of sensation, emotion, movement qualities, and impulses of the body in the current environment—you can learn to move and be moved by the awareness of the body itself.

When one relies on the mind to interpret, assume, strategize, and fantasize, *without oscillating attention back to the present-moment experience*, the mind gets swept away, increasing the chance of pushing through the discomfort of you or your partner or dissociating as your awareness drifts away from your body. When the mind is off to the races in fantasy and assumption or caught up in performative sex, boundary cues get missed, dysregulation is not identified, and the aftermath leaves sexual partners feeling resentful, disconnected, or rejected. Even though we marinate in a culture that trains us to dismiss this as normal, disregarding the present moment experience is a detriment to your connection and trust—with both yourself and each other.

These nervous system responses of pushing through, dissociating, and activating body armor are inner protectors, systems that have organized the body to survive the confusing sexuality messages that we are taught. Our bodies try their best to take care of us in the absence of more inclusive and meaningful experiences.

We are actively socialized against being in our bodies, especially in a pleasurable way. Through socialization from family, religion, and media, we learn to focus externally to align with the often-conflicting mainstream views of sex. This is a very disorienting experience. Instead of learning about what feels good to us, practicing putting accurate language to it, validating that we deserve pleasure, and then learning how to consensually engage our own desires and boundaries with a sexual intimate partner, most people spend their maturation years trying to live up to impossible standards. Our movement patterns and thoughts are focused externally on how we look, what sounds we make, how we "perform" sexually, and whether our partner is having a good time, *checking to see if we did well.* Meanwhile, autopilot habits are formed to try to meet the undeniable need for pleasure and connection in ways that keep us stagnant at best or, at worst, harm us and our relationships.

Over time, without even realizing it, resentment can build. It's inevitable. Fulfillment will never be consistent from an external source of sexual pleasure, unless we are able to oscillate inward to feel and move with and rest into the *felt sense,* or visceral feelings, of pleasure.

Bodyful intimacy is a practice—one that you get better at over time as you apply attention and *intention* in order to approach intimacy as an instrument of healing as you learn and grow together. *Whole-Body Intimacy* is a return to wildcrafting your sexual intimacy from what is true and meaningful to you and a partner in the present moment. In these chapters, you will practice *erotic bodyfulness* (see Figure 0.1)—a bodyfulness practice that guides you toward embodied and compelling pleasure. You will create structure around sensing, understanding, validating, and putting words to the emergent expressive movement of genuine pleasure and eroticism of intimacy.

This book provides information toward a paradigm shift, from centering the mind to centering the whole sensing-feeling-thinking-interacting body. It also provides a workbook of sorts where, in each chapter, you will be presented with questions to journal about and practices to do with a partner. I encourage you to take time to answer the questions and do the practices because it is in *feeling and experiencing* these concepts and practices in your physical body and in the body-to-body connection between you that the

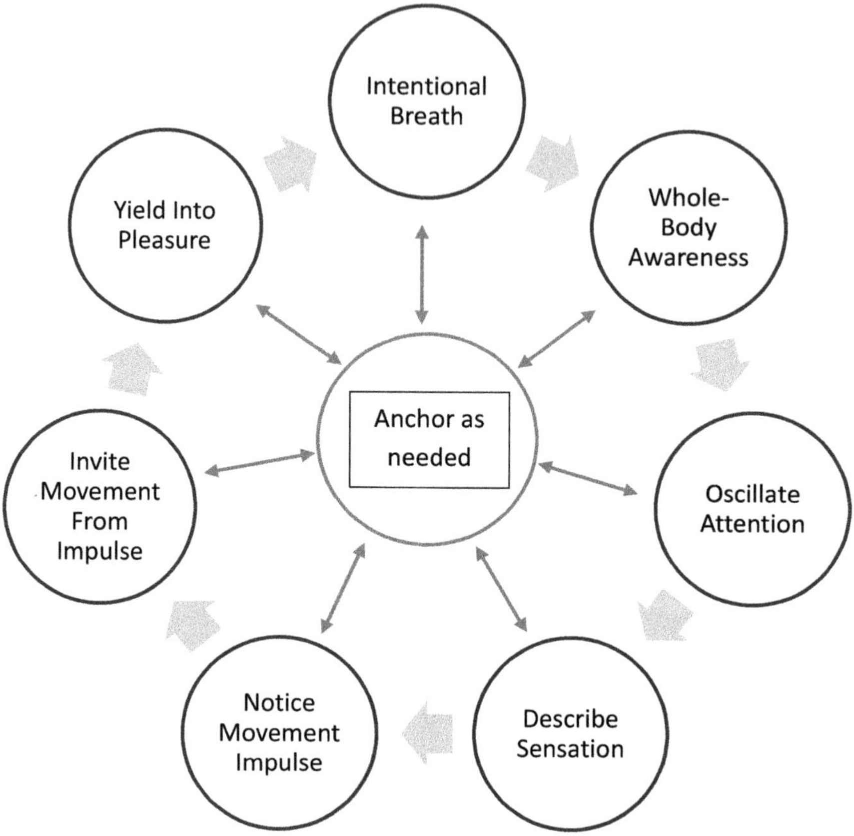

Figure 0.1 Erotic Bodyfulness Practice.

insights will appear. Incorporate the practices into your daily life so that you can give time for your relationship habits to change and take on a personal flair. It takes about a month of regular practice to change a habit, so choose one and go for it together.

Get ready to level up your intimacy!

SECTION 1

Fundamentals of a Whole-Body Intimacy

1
EMBODYING CONSENT AS A PRACTICE

Consent has been elevated in the modern spheres of sex and relationship education within the last two decades. During this time, the concept has become more nuanced and the language more descriptive—and it's about time. Not just a verbal yes and no, consent within intimacy is about prioritizing mutual, genuine pleasure, as well as being awake, aware, and attuned to emotions and physical touch in order to nourish a relationship and to heal prior relationship wounds. Consent creates the space to evolve your sexuality!

Far beyond just a gateway to sex, a consent practice invites us to set aside the unrealistic goals of a largely performative and disembodied culture. This practice is about deepening intimacy and enhancing that inner knowing of your sexual self, your arousal anatomy, and the potential of the creative, generative, and connective energy that lives within all of us.

Integrating a consent practice into your relationship is the antidote to the cultural myth that arousal and desire cannot be modulated or worked with intelligently, hence the prolific abstinence-only education and lack of national conversation about holistic sex education. The reality is that arousal and desire *can* be modulated from within. We can contain our sexual energy without shutting it down, and we can generate arousal energy without pressure. This benefits both you and your partner as you widen and deepen your capacity to be awake within arousal.

But first, we must have a clearly understood and safe-enough consent space to explore body-to-body connection that is repeatable and based on no-pressure invitations—a space that is safe enough for body awareness and experience, to be able to make mistakes, to learn, and to reconnect on a deeper level. This is the type of environment that encourages people to

DOI: 10.4324/9781003508984-3

participate, to take risks, and to be open to creativity in a more effortless and excited way.

This consent practice must involve not moving at the pace of the higher desire partner, or the partner with a clearer idea or feeling of what they want. This is also not about moving at the pace of the lower desire partner or the partner who is unclear about what they want intimately. The consent practice I present here is about *moving at the pace of connection.* This is where both people are applying awareness and intention to find the connection point between them. One of them finds what they need to yield just a bit more into the moment, while the other finds what they need to press into their edges and discover what their sexual or sensual energy needs to soften and build.

The truth is that people have different styles when it comes to expressing desire. This is completely normal—experiencing a desire difference with a partner is a challenge that arises at some point in the majority of intimate relationships.

A key to working with this dynamic in a way that supports genuine connection is the *Embodied Consent Practice.*

Consent Happens *in* the Body

Embodied consent as a repeatable practice prioritizes intimacy first. This intimacy is characterized by the presence of awareness, emotional vulnerability, safety or "safe-enough," and mutual pleasure—and informed by an intelligent relationship with arousal anatomy in the presence of another. It is an encouragement for slowness, for intentional moving and being-moved connection with self and with a partner. Embodied consent is not performative; it is *genuine.* This practice allows you to identify your autopilot reactions—automatic reactions that form from prior experiences and assumptions—in order to be more thoughtful about how you respond to your partner. Moving from the lived experience of interest, curiosity, pleasure, and intimate agreement, it makes space for both of you, moment to moment. This is the necessary antidote to rewrite the misinformed, unattainable assumptions that produce the inevitable disconnect between one's body, one's self, and one's intimate partner.

Your body, your inner landscape of sensations and breath and movement, tells you when you are feeling a *yes:* that inner lightness, inner bounce, and inner pull for connection. Your body also tells you when you are feeling a *no* or a *maybe:* that inner feeling of constriction, heaviness, or retraction away from connection. An embodied consent practice gives you the necessary pause to feel your inner yes, no, or maybe to assess what you might need in that moment to either connect with a partner or take time for yourself and return to connection later.

Let's look more closely at this process and how to apply it to get to know yourself and a partner better.

Where to Begin to Learn Embodied Consent

When I support couples to incorporate consent into their day-to-day lives, I encourage them to apply consent as a practice in many areas of their relationship—to make it a rhythm of relating that is woven into the fabric of their relationship.

Because of the complexity of sexual challenges, I find that starting with sex first can set people back. Instead, I support clients to apply embodied consent to the aspects of their relationship that comprise the ingredients of good intimacy, like communication, play and adventure, shared values, care of the home and finances, time with family and friends, sharing food, or exercising together. Take the time to consider what feels like an interesting and useful place to start your own embodied consent practice.

I'll start with a common relationship ingredient that lends itself well to learning embodied consent: everyday communication and emotional exchanges.

How many times have you or your partner launched into a story from your day before you greet your beloved or give them a chance to shift out of external world mode into intimate connection mode? You may feel as though your partner is not really listening or doesn't actually care, when in reality, they are deep in thought or still reeling from their own day. For example, when you arrive home from a long, tough day at work, instead of launching into a venting moment about your job, say to your partner: "I'd love to share about my frustrating day and hear about how your day has been. Let me know when you're available to talk," and then head upstairs to change your clothes, shower, or workout to begin moving the frustration through your body. Then, when you return downstairs to connect, your partner has had a chance to shift into a more present state to listen and connect. And you, who needed to vent, might just be a little more settled and regulated to communicate better and be more open to receiving support.

Many people don't know the emotional impact of the nervous system, or don't know that there is a range of normal when it comes to the style of connection. Because of this, you and your partner may often end up taking each other for granted, you may take your partner's responses personally or expect that your partner should have the same style as you. By omitting awareness or conversation about what kind of connection you or a partner are actually available for, you may unknowingly be opening the door to misunderstanding, hurt feelings, and missed moments of emotional intimacy. You may miss the opportunity to see and be seen by your partner because it feels like neither of you is present enough or available to bring the kind of presence and vulnerability for a nourishing exchange. We all do this because the nervous system is wired to take certain daily things for granted. Such familiarity can offer ease of connection, which can feel good and create nervous system shortcuts that conserve energy. But these assumptions and automatic body-to-body patterns can prohibit seeing and feeling each other as you are in the present moment, inhibiting fresh ways of relating and creating an obstacle to that present moment awareness that allows for the evolution of desires and boundaries across the lifespan of the connection.

The reality of human physiology is that the nervous system often needs a few moments to shift from focusing on a task to focusing on human connection. Some people make this shift with ease, while others find the transition jarring. Both are normal ways that the nervous system organizes to meet the challenges of the environment. We are in a reciprocal dance with the environment—impacting and being impacted continually—and, over time, this dance organizes the body in a way that makes you *you*. The more you get to know your *somatic architecture*—the way your muscles and tissues organize in connection with your nervous system—the more you get to know *yourself* and therefore your unique rhythm and pacing of desire, arousal, turn-ons, and turn-offs. All the better for identifying how you are feeling to more effectively express yourself and to connect with an intimate partner's somatic architecture. And all the better to notice what you need to shift from defensive or distracted to receptive and interested.

Let's look closer at nervous system states and how to recognize and advocate for what is happening beneath your skin.

Consent Supports the Health and Tone of the Nervous System

Your nervous system is the internal wiring of your body woven throughout your musculoskeletal system. It is the system that determines how you detect threat or safety (neuroception), feel and interpret environmental elements (interoception), and respond to your environment as your body experiences life and learns how to best survive and thrive in the world that you live in (expression through muscles and connective tissues that comprise the somatic nervous system). In other words, your nervous system develops certain strategies in response to the environment to get the best result.

As you move through life, your body applies what it has learned from prior experiences to current situations. Sometimes the strategy works well, and sometimes it inhibits responding appropriately. The good news is that you can get to know your strategies and learn to work *with* your nervous system to respond better in the moment. Because sexuality is highly socialized, your nervous system develops strategies in response to body-to-body intimate connection. Therefore, your early learning about touch, body autonomy, or how love is expressed organizes your nervous system responses so that your body applies this knowledge to your adult intimate relationships.

Based on the *Polyvagal Theory* by psychiatrist Stephen Porges, two nervous system strategies are identified, neurobiological processes "which have evolved into an integrated neurobehavioral system, which promotes proximity, reproduction, and physical safety" (Porges, 2011, 166). One nervous system strategy facilitates closeness and intimacy, while the other nervous system strategy supports retreat from social contact to recharge or protect. We can learn to identify and modulate these two strategies in ourselves to modulate and improve how we engage in intimacy.

You can identify that the *Social Engagement System* (SES) is active in your body when you feel open and excited for connection. You are able to express your thoughts and feelings while presenting as alert and awake. While in your SES, you are also more open to hearing about a partner's experience and to understanding what makes sense about what they are feeling, even if you don't resonate with their experience at that moment.

The SES also supports accessing pleasure in intimate connection. Sex Educator Emily Nagoski renames the SES as the Sexual Excitation System (2015), which highlights the connection between the nervous system and arousal anatomy. Feeling safe enough in proximity and interested in closeness triggers the simultaneous release of oxytocin (a hormone and neuropeptide that supports social bonding, stress relief, sexual arousal, and even lactation) and vasopressin (a hormone that works as a vasodilator, increasing heart rate), which activates both relaxation and excitement at the same time. This promotes prosocial behaviors and initiates the increase in intensity of arousal, pleasure, and, if safety, pleasure and excitement continue to build, orgasm. Also, since "vestibular stimulation elicits systemic vasopressin release" (Porges, 175), pleasurable movement such as dance or swinging on a swing in proximity to an intimate partner can elicit the experience of passionate arousal or love.

You can also identify when you feel tension in your muscles, an uncomfortable intensity, and a desire for decreased proximity when the *Social Inhibition System* (SIS) is active. This is where your partner's proximity feels less tolerable or downright activating to you. You will have less patience, less openness, and a desire to distract, disconnect, or isolate. Your SIS is telling you that you need to take care of your nervous system by being alone in a hot bath, or getting a loving hug, or sitting in a low-stimulation environment, whatever helps to reduce distress, so that your nervous system can regulate itself. Nagoski (2015) renames the SIS as the *Sexual Inhibition System*. The relative immobilization characteristic of sex through sustained body contact can activate a feeling of fear when the SIS and not the SES is active. This then activates the fight, flight, or freeze response, based on how your body has adapted to mobilizing in the presence of danger or perceived threat. Relative immobilization when the Social/Sexual Engagement/Excitation System is active promotes what Porges calls the *immobilization love system,* which is "physiologically and psychologically incompatible with the immobilized fear system" (Porges, 181), which is the system that activates when the Social/Sexual Inhibition System is online.

Both of these states are responses to your environment—the context (environment and social situation) that you just came from impacts the current context and combines with the belief system and strategies that you learned in your early life. Your body picks up information from the environment through your *exteroceptive senses,* while your *interoceptive senses* tell you how your environment is impacting how you feel inside your body. Your nervous system begins to shift state from the combination of these senses as messages are sent to your brain to interpret and apply beliefs to explain why you are feeling the way that you do.

When the environment invites the SES state to activate, you are relaxed and at ease in your body. You can communicate how you are feeling and be attentive as a partner shares their feelings. Overall, connection feels good, welcome, and nourishing. In the SES state, you are also within your *window of capacity* and better able to deal with difficulty as your nervous system is regulated and responsive.

When the environment causes the SIS state to activate, either from a sudden stressor or through stress building over time, you will feel a range of uncomfortable feelings, from irritability to wanting to run out of a room or to hide. The SIS is an overstimulated and dysregulated state, and you will greatly benefit from reducing stimulation by leaving a social situation to regulate or spending time in a quiet room with very little stimulation. Think of a time when overwhelm inspired you to literally put your head under a blanket. Human contact becomes simply too much, and time is needed to quietly regulate the nervous system before returning to human contact to effectively, maybe joyfully, interact with others.

For most people, the activation of the SIS initially causes them to drop into *autopilot* behaviors, which are the unconscious ways that we find to just try to feel better but are not actually nourishing and regulating to the nervous system. Autopilot behaviors can be checking out by phone scrolling, eating, or substance use, like drinking alcohol. They can also be sensation-seeking for physical release. These behaviors engage in physical intensity, like sex, to release the tension in their body and find relaxation.

Overall, the SIS is an inner *no,* a state of dysregulation (either low intensity or high intensity), and the body naturally seeks something to help return to regulation.

Another important feature of the SIS is that when your body experiences this dysregulation, you are operating from your *dorsal vagal complex (DVC),* a sensory relay station found in the brain stem that regulates visceral sensory processing such as taste, blood pressure, and information from the lungs and gut. This is the vestige of our reptilian origins that is instinctual and reactive. The DVC is tasked with keeping us safe, alerting us to danger, and escaping pain. When the SIS is active, the forebrain, the part of the brain that allows us to be awake and aware of ourselves and others and to hold multiple perspectives, has far less activity. As you can probably guess, when we approach sexual connection while you or a partner is in their SIS state, the connection is more likely to be rife with misunderstanding, reactivity, defense, and greater difficulty navigating conscious consent. When one feels threatened (which is not the intention of the intimate partner but is coded as such when the nervous system is in an SIS state), body-to-body contact or even the presence of a partner's arousal can feel threatening. As a professor of psychiatry, Judith Herman says, "Traumatic symptoms have a tendency to become disconnected from their source and to take on a life of their own" (Herman, 1992, 34).

The good news is that you can get better at regulating your nervous system when you identify the SIS state and begin to heal past relational trauma. As you refine the skills of awareness, you can get better at waking up from the autopilot behaviors and instead choose to engage in more nourishing behaviors that help your body discharge the intensity and return to more SES functioning. By refining your ability to identify when you are in your SES and SIS, you can better support your body to shift from inhibition to excitation and receptivity to sexual intimacy.

This is where the embodied consent practice is particularly useful. It inserts a pause between the impulse or invitation for sex and the response or action so that you offer yourself and your partner the space to check in with your body and notice what is needed to shift into receptivity—from inhibition to excitation.

Similar to the dance/movement therapy practice of Authentic Movement (Pallaro, 1999), a body-based movement meditation that centers deep witnessing of the many layers of yourself, embodied consent encourages you to move at the pace of *moving and being moved at the same time*. This requires a slowness of awareness that allows you to put a gap between impulse and action, to express from genuine desire, and also be able to track your partner.

Embodied Consent Builds Trust

If I were to pose the question of what makes for good sex, you might think of things such as *passion, mystery, primal desire*, and so on. And, sure, these things can feel really great once arousal has built in intensity and connection feels genuine. But consider this: can you build desire and intense passion *without feeling safe enough*? As we saw earlier, a safe-enough proximity is vital to deep intimacy and pleasure.

Many people have not had their body autonomy respected in their life, and therefore their somatic "no" becomes stronger than their "yes." If you notice that your body expresses more tension and retraction within an initiation for intimacy, you probably have had people disrespect or violate your body boundaries in some way.

Embodied consent is a practice that creates a structure for a *secure attachment rhythm* in your relationship. An important feature of secure attachment in human-to-human connection is a sense of trust that allows you both to have space to be individual humans in the world who are interconnected, without losing body autonomy, while benefiting from mutual support and connection. But trust is not a given, and it is not a solid state—it is actually a *rhythm,* a sequence of actions or phrasing you express with each other that, as you repeat, gains more stability over time. The rhythm of trust is created through the sequence of: sharing a feeling/desire/need, your partner validating that feeling/desire/need, appreciating and breathing in the nourishment of emotional and/or physical contact, and regardless of whether your partner does or doesn't share your feeling/desire/need, validating them in return.

When enacting the rhythm of trust as a practice, you and your partner can learn what your body needs to soften without obligation or force. The most important part of embodied consent as a practice is that it removes the expectation of a particular goal and instead centers connection. It prioritizes consensual agreement based on how both people *are* feeling in the present moment, instead of putting pressure on how they *should* feel.

Let's begin with a prerequisite practice to lay the foundation for embodied consent.

Body Autonomy Practice—A Prerequisite to Embodied Consent

Sit or stand across from your partner as you determine a proximity that allows you to both be in connection with yourself (awareness of what you are feeling and expressing) and also be in connection with your partner—think connection without touch, within emotional kinesphere versus physical kinesphere. Choose who will be partner A and who will be partner B.

Now, take a few full in-breaths followed by long out-breaths and find a meaningful somatic sensation by asking yourself how it feels to sit/stand across from your intimate partner. Do you notice softening and open sensations or tightening/constricting sensations or both? Just notice the inner sensations and breath around them to give the sensations and their movement qualities the space that they need. Now, partner A, reduce proximity by taking a step back from your partner. When partner A shifts their body back, partner B takes a deep breath in and intentionally tells them, "I trust your body autonomy." *Partner A, notice what happens to your inner sensations when your partner says this—do they stay the same, or change? You can ask partner B to repeat this phrase a few times to notice very closely how your body responds, awakening those deeper brain structures. If partner A has experienced past sexual trauma, you can add,* "Your comfort is more important than my arousal." *Partner A, notice what happens in your inner landscape when partner B shares this. Take a few moments to share what you notice and, when you are ready, switch roles so that partner B is the one who moves back and receives the* "I trust your body autonomy" statement.

And remember that if your partner says that they internally relaxed with less proximity, you don't have to take this personally! It is difficult for some people to soften initially with closeness due to their nervous system and/or prior experiences.

This may be the first time that someone has said that they honor your bodily autonomy. Allow any emotion that comes up to move your body, your tears, and your anger—then, after the emotion has moved your body, come back to stillness and check in by asking yourself what you notice now. Do you feel the same or different from before? Resource by getting an icepack from the freezer and placing it on your cheeks, neck, or chest; go for a brisk walk; get a cup of tea and meditate; do something that meets the intensity in your body, and then follow the impulse to intentionally release and relax.

Acknowledging each other's body autonomy is a fundamental understanding that makes embodied consent both relevant and meaningful. It also sets the stage for greater desire, as connection with individuality supports attraction.

Embodied Consent Increases Pleasure

Embodied consent practice establishes a space to move at the pace of the body, so that you can move directly from that inner interest to lean toward what genuinely feels pleasurable. This allows space to express pleasure-based movement. You are more likely to move in pleasurable ways when you know that your partner honors your body autonomy and is a safe-enough person to be intimately vulnerable with.

A body that can feel safe enough to move with the sensations of pleasure is a body that gets to embrace the inner *yes* with autonomy and agency. You have arrived in that consensual erotic space when you and your partner can physically connect in a mutual pleasure-based *yes*. Touch takes consent to a whole new level.

Sex educator Dr. Betty Martin (2021) encourages people to increase awareness and intentionality with physical connection and touch. With her *Wheel of Consent,* Martin encourages people to ask the questions, "Who is doing the touch?" and "Who is the touch *for?*" She identifies four intersecting quadrants in her wheel: within "who is doing the touch," the two quadrants are "I touch you the way *you* want" (serving/giving touch) or "I touch you the way *I* want" (taking touch); And within "who is the touch for," the two quadrants are "you touch me the way *you* want" (allowing touch) or "you touch me the way *I* want" (accepting/receiving touch). These quadrants have both light and shadow qualities (e.g., giving/serving touch could be genuine enjoyment in giving or resentful people pleasing). Embodied consent is a key to clarifying what you and a partner are feeling and what kind of touch you are genuinely interested in engaging in at the present time in the present context. Putting a pause between impulse and action allows you to navigate any arousal non-concordance and touch or receive touch from any of the four quadrants in a way that feels attuned and genuinely interesting.

Embodied consent, plus intentionality and excitement, creates a space where you get to experience that flow state within and between you. The flow state is also referred to as *being in the zone*, where your attention is completely absorbed with the activity you are doing, letting go of a sense of time and space. This is a moment of *transcendence*.

The Practice of Embodied Consent

Overall, the rhythm goes like this: check in with self, connect with partner, and pause. Over time, you will incorporate this practice into your own style, allowing the practice to feel more organic and less artificially structured.

- You want to initiate intimate contact with your partner.
- Then check in with yourself: what is your nervous system state (SES or SIS)? From where within yourself are you wanting to reach for your partner (from desire, from anxiousness, or from obligation)? Does the quality of your desire to reach have an energy of serving/giving touch, or is the energy more about taking touch? Do you feel grounded in the present moment? Do you feel attuned—connected with both yourself and the emotional and somatic state of your intimate partner—in the present moment with your partner?
- Share with your partner your interest in connection/touch/physical intimacy and where you are connecting from within yourself. Pause.
- Notice how the receiving partner responds. Does their body tense up? Does their breathing become tight? Or does their body soften and breathe deeper? If they tense up, don't take it personally. Their context may or may not support intimacy at this moment, so this is where you give *them* time to check in with themselves to see if they are available or interested in contact.
- Tell your partner that you trust their body autonomy.

- Check in with how they are doing. Don't ask *what is wrong.* Just ask something like, *how are you feeling* or *would you like to slow down?* Discuss with each other to find language that feels good to both of you.
- Partner, you get to respond here! Take your time to see how their desire/invitation feels to you. Do you notice an inner yes (softening, opening, leaning toward, or pleasant bubbling)? Do you notice an inner *no* (tightening to your midline, constriction in muscles or chest, leaning away, or uncomfortable inner shaking)? Or both? How might your context (your physical environment, social environment, recent events, etc.) be impacting you in this moment?
- Partner, ask yourself, *what do I need to soften my no?* Share with the initiating partner what you notice and what would be helpful for you to connect or if you are not currently available or interested in contact, and would like to reconnect at a different time.
- Once you do what you think could be helpful, check in again. *Do I feel the same or different?* If you are ready, invite or initiate contact.
- Repeat as needed!

Questions to explore together:

- What are the social and physical environmental conditions that activate your Social or Sexual Engagement/Excitation System?
- What are the social and physical environmental conditions that activate your Social or Sexual Inhibition System?
- What helps your body shift out of your SIS and back into present moment awareness?

2
EMBODYING COMMUNICATION

I'll let you in on a little secret.

Sometimes, your partner goes to bed early because they want you to follow them upstairs for intimacy. Sometimes, your partner hugs you in a sensual way without expecting sex. Sometimes, your partner asks you to cuddle in bed because they want to just cuddle, but other times, they are hoping that their arousal anatomy will come online. And sometimes, maybe often, you and your partner mean different things when you talk or hint about having sex.

In all cases, the possibility of misunderstanding, feeling rejected, feeling a sense of not being seen, or feeling not being desired increases when you or your partner doesn't check in with each other about your assumptions.

Imagine all the missed opportunities for connection!

Yet, how would you know about these missed opportunities if you are not coming from a shared understanding or shared meaningfulness of sex and intimacy? And how would you know if this is not being spoken?

These are the types of scenarios that I often hear in my couples therapy practice when I begin to investigate the relationship dynamic as I invite each person to share how *they* feel they express intimate or sexual feelings. The reality is, there is no *one right way*, although the media often gives you the message that there is (i.e., you must sound sultry or confident or aloof or whatever). Surrounded by confusing messages about sexual intimacy, the cards are stacked against people being transparent in a meaningful and relational way. It is difficult to just be yourself as you are, and it is common to find that you are minimizing your expression. This often doubles down on any body armor (patterns of muscle tension, retraction, and discomfort in your somatic architecture) that you carry from your childhood or prior relationships.

DOI: 10.4324/9781003508984-4

More than likely, your partner is not intentionally withholding connection or intentionally being unclear about their verbal or physical communication. It's just that they are unsure about *what* to communicate or *how* to communicate in a way that lands well, honors both of you, and fits within the amount of time that is given for connection. Their body armor, just like yours, is inhibiting *them* from expressing themselves.

Many people don't even have a language for intimacy that feels meaningful and doesn't spark embarrassment or shame. For many, the language of sexuality comes from the anatomical language found in sex education, the "dirty talk" from pornography, or the pop-culture language found in lifestyle magazines. It is challenging to understand ourselves and find accurate and meaningful words when our emergent thoughts and feelings are running through the ill-fitting and confusing social-sexual filters. So, instead of diving into this complexity in real time, many people automatically simplify the process by simply not bringing it up or relying on euphemisms. This is the relationship protection setting of the nervous system.

Not talking about sex and intimacy leaves too much room for false narratives. You end up moving through your relationship holding parallel narratives based on assumptions about yourself and your partner. One person may be thinking that all the stars must align for their partner to say yes to sexual intimacy, while the other may think that if they ask for something different this time, their partner will be disappointed or reject them. This can be uncomfortable and underscores a lack of trust in your ability to communicate clearly with each other about your sex life.

Much of the language to initiate sexual intimacy or talk about it with partners falls in the category of euphemisms. A euphemism, as defined by the Oxford dictionary, is "a mild or indirect word or expression substituted for one considered to be too harsh or blunt when referring to something unpleasant or embarrassing." One of my client couples would say, "I'm going up for a shower," or another couple would often suggest, "let's go to bed early" to hint at being ready for sex. Using euphemisms for sex sometimes creates ease in avoiding the discomfort of being direct, but more often creates misunderstanding and discomfort. When you are learning and refining your communication about sexual intimacy, there are benefits and drawbacks to euphemistic flirting versus mind–body congruent expression. Flirting can be fun and playful, but when it comes to actual sexual activity and boundaries when you don't have a safe-enough shared reality and language about sex, I encourage people to opt for being more direct: hints and euphemisms don't support your goal of rewriting assumptions and outdated patterns or expanding the realm of sexual intimacy with a partner.

While it is true that there is no one right way to express intimate thoughts and feelings, it does matter that it is spoken aloud and in connection with the body, specifically in a way that aligns with what you are actually feeling in the moment, complexity and all. Your partner needs you to be clear and descriptive while sharing in digestible pieces. It is easy to misinterpret words and gestures as a result of the confusing messages that you absorbed about sexuality within the context of relationships as you grew up. Overall, our culture, even still in 2025, does a terrible job teaching us about sex and how to talk to each other about it. Excellent education exists these days from educators and counselors such as Emily Nagoski, Sheri Winston, Laurie Mintz, Marty Klein, or Barry McCarthy, to name a few, though you have to actively seek it out from your own interest—usually at the time when a difficulty or relationship wound has already happened, not before. This makes learning about sexuality and accepting the humanness of you and your partner a bit more challenging.

By the time you have arrived in your adult, intimate relationship, you have well-worn paths in your mind and habits in your nervous system about what sex is, what your automatic pace and rhythm is, and how to approach or avoid it, so there is some serious swimming-up-stream learning to be done. This process can be challenging, but also exciting and revelatory. After all, talking about your sexual intimacy is a form of sexual intimacy itself!

When stepping into a more honest and descriptive way of communicating, a fundamental skill that will increase your chance of success is to own your own communication style. Owning and naming your part in this dynamic is key. This is a moment of radical acceptance of each of your humanness and how you both contribute to the challenges. This is not about blame or fault—this is about recognizing that both of you brought beliefs and ways of relating from your lived experience that will benefit from some creative remodeling. You don't necessarily mean to make assumptions about each other or hurt each other's feelings, yet that is what happens as a normal part of a relationship.

By *owning* your side of things, you are normalizing that intimate relationships are an ongoing embodied creative practice, and you are empowering yourself to be at your best in this process. Participating with honest self-reflection and a learning mind is humbling, exhilarating, and the foundation of a healthy relationship. It is okay to say, *I notice I become defensive/shutdown/talk faster, etc. when x,y,z happens* . . . And then think about what would be helpful (what you can do first, then ask for support from your partner) for you to soften the nervous system dysregulation in the moment.

Unpacking Assumptions to Get to the Need Underneath

Assumptions are normal mechanisms of the mind that we develop to more efficiently interpret and respond to the world. In an intimate relationship, assumptions help us to have an understanding of a partner and the relationship dynamic so that we don't have to reinvent the wheel every day. This is what John Gottman called the *Love Map* (2015), the map in your mind that holds your understanding of your relationship. Assumptions develop from the empathic experience of our relational neurophysiology—from our ability to detect what others are feeling. Yet, when we sense what is happening for our partner, we are running it through our own filters, perspective, and experience. So, without verbal confirmation from our partner, we make assumptions and run with them.

For example, you know that most days your partner likes a cup of coffee, so every morning you make a pot for two. This can be a sweet gesture that you will get right most of the time. If your partner wakes up one day and says they prefer green tea or a smoothie, it probably won't be a big deal to widen your assumption to include this new information.

But what if you have an assumption about how your partner likes to be touched during sexual intimacy? They communicated verbally and/or nonverbally in past intimate experiences that they enjoyed your light touch along their back or firm pressure on their legs, so why do they seem not to enjoy it at this moment? Seeing the assumption as fact could take you down a rabbit hole of questioning whether they are attracted to you anymore, whether they enjoy sex with you anymore, and so on. When actually, it could be that the light touch or firm pressure is only really enjoyable to them *when they are already aroused,* and when they are *not* aroused, it feels overstimulating.

The target of assumptions goes both ways. You probably have some assumptions about yourself that are getting in the way of embodied intimacy. Take a moment to consider. Do you assume that you are supposed to enjoy a certain kind of touch or certain sexual activities? Or maybe you have assumptions about what an orgasm is supposed to feel like or how quickly your arousal anatomy should get turned on.

The roots of assumptions and how you respond to them often originate from lived experience *prior* to your relationship. You probably have underlying beliefs about how a good partner behaves, like thoughtfully making coffee in the morning, or about what makes a good sexual connection, like knowing what your partner wants without them telling you. I find that many of the assumptions related to sexual intimacy are actually not true—often, the source material is a movie they saw as a young person, what they witnessed in their parents' relationship, or sex education 101 circa seventh grade. These assumptions often contain their own defense mechanisms and body armor, making exploring and questioning even more challenging.

The point is not about whether your assumption is right or wrong, but it's about being present for the intimacy of the moment and asking yourself or a partner whether the assumption is true. Get curious about where this assumption came from and ask your body, *what is actually true in this moment, in this context.* Then take the time to communicate to your partner your feeling, your desire, while *being open to learning something new about each other and yourself.*

When you notice an assumption arises in your mind, turn it into a genuine question. Tell your partner, *I notice that I'm having this assumption.* Once you share the assumption, ask them, *did I get that right?* Give your partner time to consider and respond. If your partner shares a feeling that is difficult to hear or feels like an assumption, share the gratitude and then ask questions, such as *tell me more about feeling taken for granted.*

Questioning your assumptions about intimacy and about your intimate partner requires owning that this is your own interpretation, and a willingness to shift your perspective from the rigidity of assumptions to an interested and learning state of mind.

In Dance/Movement Therapy terms, we call this shifting into a *learning pre-effort state* (Amighi et al., 2018). Pre-effort is a mind–body state that we enter when we are learning something new or defending against something threatening, depending on the context. When in pre-effort, the body and mind are not fully coordinated. You can feel awkward, uncertain, silly, and defensive—all the feelings that the dominant culture often defines as categorically *unsexy.*

When the pre-effort state is coupled with a lack of safety or openness, you can feel your body armor being activated. This is a *defending pre-effort* state where you are more likely to feel rigid and internally retracted, breathing more shallow, and having thoughts that sound more critical and, you guessed it, full of assumptions.

However, when you feel safe enough and you and your partner are open to being curious and uncertain, you know that you are in a *learning* pre-effort state. While in a learning pre-effort state and the context is supportive, you may feel awkward and hesitant, and you may laugh or cry to release any tension. This can feel fun, interesting, and deeply emotional, like learning something new about a fascinating and meaningful subject.

Taking time to explore in the learning pre-effort state as a goal unto itself makes it possible to discover emergent feelings, desire, pleasure, and ways of connecting that you hadn't noticed before. Be willing to be surprised and delighted by what you learn about yourself and your intimate partner.

You can work together to create the conditions that make a learning pre-effort state more likely. Step 1 is to take context into consideration and to co-create a supportive environment to learn embodied intimate communication.

Embodied Communication

It is the congruence between what you are feeling and what you are saying moment to moment while moving at the pace of connection with each other that helps you build shared language and values. This is *embodied communication,* and it supports clarity, a greater sense of trust, and connection.

Step 1: Context Impacts Everything

Your environment, both social and physical, impacts your body directly, influencing whether you are open to learning and exploring or you are closed off to the present moment. You may not realize in the moment that your nervous system is dysregulated and therefore more likely to make assumptions that disconnect you from your partner, yourself, and the present moment. You have probably received the message to *just get over it,* not to make a big deal about how you feel. Honestly, this simply doesn't work most of the time. When just getting over it *does* work, it usually requires disconnecting your emotions from the situation and the people around you to do it. Not a good recipe for intimacy.

The reality is that you can indeed tolerate uncomfortable emotions enough, within your window of capacity, to feel what you are feeling and share your experience descriptively with a partner. Remember that embodied consent practice? Now is the moment that you get to slow down and consider how the environment is impacting you and how your partner's context is impacting them, to notice what you might need in order to shift your mental and physical state into the present moment—to soften, to feel excited and interested in connection.

When practicing embodied communication, you are invited to slow down enough to consider the following:

- What kind of day have I had? Stressful? Relaxing?
- How do I feel about the current environment? Am I distracted by the mess or uncomfortable with the temperature?
- What do I notice in my body? Are there places of tension or discomfort? How might I describe them?
- How do I feel about our connection at this moment? Are we both able to be present and open for connection, or are we distracted and stressed?
- What makes sense about the assumption that I'm having? Where did I learn it?
- What resources could help me/us learn about alternatives to the assumption?

Now, you can create the context that allows you to be in a learning mind together. Share with each other:

- What do I need to feel safe enough?
- What would help me relax and shake off my stressful day?
- How do I describe what I'm feeling/wanting in sensation/feeling language?

One of the things that I notice the most when working with couples is that partners often have different styles of relating, which is normal and not necessarily a problem when they have a good sense of how to work together while honoring each other's needs.

What do you find that you need in order to be present for an intimate conversation? Some people need time to themselves first to unwind—to go for a walk, take a hot shower, or eat some good food. Other people want to have some time to connect with their partner first—to go for a walk together, eat food together, or talk about their day. Couples therapist Brent Atkinson (2005) calls this difference togetherness first versus independence first. Atkinson speaks about how this can be challenging, but totally workable:

> *If two people who are wired more for independence are paired in a relationship, they can function just fine, and so can two people who are more wired for togetherness. Mismatches are difficult, but most relationships are mismatched, at least to a degree, and mismatched relationships thrive under the right conditions. What are these conditions? You each accept the idea that both of your nervous systems have legitimate ways of stabilizing, and you each stretch your own comfort levels a bit so you're able to give and take in a way where each of you gets your needs at least partially met.*
>
> *(Atkinson, version 4.1)*

An intentional transition practice makes space for differences in processing and communication styles, allowing equitable validation of feelings and space for each other's humanness.

Intentional Transition

The *Intentional Transition Practice* is a practice that I encourage my clients to incorporate into their daily life. It invites a pause at the beginning of your day, when you arrive home from work, or before you go to bed—whenever it feels more important to include a decelerated moment to connect. The intentional transition provides a structure to check in with yourself first and then with your partner as you consider the impact of context—your physical and social environment—on your nervous system and what assumptions are being triggered. This practice is, at times, like building a strong boat to carry you over potentially rough waters or, at other times, like laying down in a warm grassy field together. It serves as a time-out of time to facilitate a better entry into the next moment.

Take a moment to sit across from your partner as I guide you through the practice.

Practice: Intentional Transition

Sit or stand facing your partner. Soften your gaze or close your eyes. Take a full breath in—expanding your ribcage, belly, and back body—and a long breath out, softening muscles and bones. Take another full breath in—expanding your torso and sequencing out through your arms and legs with a stretch, opening the fascia around your muscles—and a long breath out, widening your hips over your seat, widening the bottoms of your feet over the floor.

As you breathe in and breathe out, invite your awareness inward to notice your somatosensory awareness within your body. Allow your awareness to be like a bird, gently flying over the inner somatic landscape of your body, noticing the different landmarks of sensation but not attaching to any. You may notice a place of tightness here and a place of openness there, a place of pain or discomfort, and a place that is asking for the support of a pillow or a hand. These are the echoes within your body from the context that you just came from—this is what you have brought into the room with you. Echoes of your job, traffic, a massage, cooking dinner, or scrolling on your phone—whatever you had been doing before you sat down.

If there are places of tension, allow your awareness to settle in and around this place, surrounding it with breath and asking it, what does it want you to know? After breathing in a breath of gratitude for your body sharing with you, thanking this sensation for telling you how it feels or reminding you of something important, ask it what it needs to be able to soften, to land in this moment with your partner. Perhaps it needs something immediate, a warm cup of tea to hold in your hands, or another pillow to increase physical comfort. Perhaps it needs something else, like for you to go take a shower, or change your clothes after work, or to hear that your partner is pleased to see you. Make note of what it tells you.

As you breathe in what your body has shared, notice if the sensation feels the same or different. Invite your body to follow any micromovements that begin to happen from the origin of the sensation that you feel. Perhaps a stretch of your neck side to side begins to happen, or a twist of your spine, a yawn, or a swaying/rocking back and forth. Allow yourself to follow the rhythm and direction that your body is expressing.

Take one more full breath in and a full breath out, and, when you are ready, find your partner's eyes and/or hear their breath and feel their presence near you. Notice how it is to see them and/or to feel their presence in front of you.

Take turns sharing the echoes that you noticed within your somatic landscape and what you may need to land more fully with your partner and into the rest of your day. Share your experience in as descriptive words as you possible (sensation, movement quality, metaphor), and maybe even share your movement with your partner. Once your partner shares, say "thank you for telling me," and then share your own.

Once both of you have shared, notice how you feel toward them now—do you notice an inner lean that is encouraging you to ask for a hug or a kiss, or do you notice a desire to go to the thing that your body asked for before dropping in with your partner? Remember that you have different nervous systems that may need different things to land, so thank your partner for sharing what they need/want and invite both of you to follow the impulse. Then, if your intentional transition precedes time you get to spend together, return to connection.

Step 2: Speak Descriptively in Mind–Body Alignment

Speaking descriptively requires some bravery and strong self-compassion. Yet using descriptive language within mind–body alignment provides an opportunity to rewire your internal understanding of sexuality, and to begin to identify the internal contradictions that have caused any prior misunderstandings, which led to painful breaches of body boundaries or relationship agreements. This takes practice because humans often rely on a shorthand way of communicating that prevents us from revealing vulnerable sensations and feelings. In a society that is often hostile toward sexuality and vulnerable feelings, it makes sense that our language serves to protect us in this way. If you didn't have a safe-enough place in your life growing up to share feelings and hear others' feelings with an undefended heart, now is the opportunity to cultivate this with your intimate partner. Embodied communication creates the opportunity to feel the essence of intimacy—to see and be seen.

Focus your inner awareness with curiosity and openness on your inner landscape with descriptive, somatic-based language. As we have discussed, being as descriptive as possible sidesteps the big assumptions and defensiveness that come with labels while offering equal validation that helps a partner to feel safe enough and interested to connect. It conveys to a partner that you are aware of your own experience and that there is also room for their experience to exist, allowing body armor to soften and a sense of closeness to begin to unfurl.

Descriptive language—the language of sensation (texture, temperature, size, shape), movement quality, and body physics—allows your partner to feel you in 3D so that somatic empathy can create connection and attunement between you. Somatic empathy is a subjective experience where you have a felt-sense of your partner's experience. By both feeling and descriptively hearing about your partner's experience, you are less likely to ascribe meaning to their experience from your perspective. I often hear people tell their partner something like, "I feel like you don't want to be intimate because you are overstretching yourself at your job." They say that they can feel their partner's exhaustion and distraction. But even when some version of the assumption is correct, it still often feels disconnecting to hear your partner's interpretation. It's more important and more connecting to have felt-sense of your partner's experience and ask them, "I notice that you seem tired during our window for intimacy—does that feel true?" This allows you to feel your partner and also let them be the expert of their own experience.

You have probably known your intimate partner for some time, so you probably have associations related to the words that they chose to use and what you think they mean by them. These assumptions, as we've discussed, are from a familiarity between you. They form the shortcuts that we gather as we get to know someone. However, these assumptions may not be helpful as you invest in feeling that spark of present-moment intimacy with them. Allow yourself to be fascinated by the words and gestures they express to describe their experience.

Descriptive words can describe the dimensions of sensation such as texture (like smooth, rough, scratchy, bumpy, and sticky), temperature (like warm, tepid, hot, and frosty), size (like large, narrow, small, and long), shape (like round, rectangular, spiky, and wall-like), weight qualities (like light and heavy), and movement qualities (like spreading/widening, shrinking, bubbling, shaking, dropping/melting, and rising/evaporating).

By investing in descriptive language, you open up a whole landscape of possibilities within you. When you pause before responding to your partner, take a full breath in and a long breath out, and notice how your body has been impacted by your context or by your partner's sharing. You have the opportunity to feel their words echoing within you. The places where your body softens and opens are the places where their words and experience have been *received*. The places where your body tightens are the places that resist receiving—these are the areas that let you know that you might need further clarification, where perhaps a misunderstanding or old wound exists.

I encourage my clients to take their time here and not use this inner tightening as a blank to fill in by either disconnecting or *performing* intimacy and connection out of obligation—that is not true intimacy. Instead, share with your partner the complexity that you feel. On one hand, you feel a softening (be descriptive), and at the same time, you feel a tightening (be descriptive). Both you and your partner will benefit from making space for each other's humanness and the complexity that comes with being in a human body in a relationship. Thank your partner for sharing the complexity! Sharing gratitude shifts you into a learning pre-effort state as you navigate challenging moments together. This is true intimacy. Having enough trust in the structure of your body and your relationship to hold this complexity with closeness and openness.

It's okay if the expression begins with *I don't know what I feel*—think of this as a loading screen. It takes time and focused attention to discern what is being felt and to find the descriptive language to allow your partner to feel you and settle into somatic empathy together. If finding the sensations and language feels easy for you, make sure that you slow down and embrace your partner if they have a longer loading screen. It will be worth it!

Step 3: Feel What You Say as You Say It

To take this interaction to the deeper layers, the skill of *feeling what you say as you say it* allows the body to communicate the meaningfulness of what is being said on a visceral level. The feeling that is being transmitted then impacts the somatic experience of the partner. I like to call this *communicating at the pace of your body*. If you can't feel what you are saying as you say it, you're going too fast.

It's okay that your mind may not understand it all in the moment. Instead, allow yourself to return to the present moment and trust that the cognitive or intellectual meaning will form over a period of time. To come to a conclusion too quickly allows assumptions to creep back in.

Instead, oscillate your attention to connect with what you are feeling in your own body, sharing descriptive words—*I notice that I feel (sensation) in this moment*—then oscillate your attention to your partner so they can reflect what they heard you say and share what makes sense about why you are feeling that in this moment.

For example, my clients Cynthia and Ryan came into session wanting to talk about what happened over the weekend. Ryan began talking first. Cynthia became overwhelmed as her partner, Ryan, shared his experience of their intimacy over the weekend. I noticed her body becoming quite still while he was speaking, her muscles presenting more rigid and tightly pulled into her midline. Since Ryan had not been looking at Cynthia during his sharing, he was not aware that her nervous system had shifted, so I invited them to slow down, turn to face each other, and begin with an intentional transition. I guided them through the practice that I detailed earlier, and Cynthia began sharing first. I encouraged her to feel what she was saying as she spoke. She closed her eyes, put her hand over her chest, and said that when Ryan spoke about their intimacy, she began to feel a tightening in her belly and a tension in her throat. She spoke slowly and paused between each statement to reconnect with the sensation. She connected these feelings to the way he seemed to be assuming her experience. As Ryan listened to Cynthia, I noticed he tensed up at first, but as she slowed down and shared descriptively what her body was feeling, he softened and leaned toward her. "Thanks for sharing that," he said, "it makes sense that my assuming your experience was uncomfortable." She appreciated his acknowledging that and encouraged him to keep sharing about their experience but to check with her when he had an assumption.

I asked them later what happened for them here, and Ryan shared that because she was saying what she was feeling, he could tell that she wasn't blaming him, just sharing impact. This made a hard thing to hear more bearable, and he was able to access a feeling of empathy and compassion.

Speak From Your Desire

Now that you have the skill to feel what you say as you speak, you can apply this to moments of initiating intimacy. This supports speaking directly from the inner sensation of your own desire with mind–body alignment, with description, while making space for your partner's experience. It is time to own your own interest: instead of saying "would you like to be intimate later?" say "I would love to have some intimacy later, are you interested?" and to notice from where within yourself you are speaking from: an anxious place? A defensive place? An excited place? A place that longs for connection or a place that expects to be disappointed? Invite in that breath and recognize that your desire is wonderful, and your partner may or may not be open to intimacy in that moment, but sharing your desire is a moment of intimacy that feeds the larger garden of your relationship. Speak descriptively, feeling as you speak, as you tell your partner something like, "as I see you sitting over there, I notice that I feel a warmth in my body and I would really love to hold you." While you may want a full sexual intimacy experience, when there is no expectation beyond this initial expression and invitation, your partner may be more inclined to feel warmth in return and a mutual desire for contact. The partner may then check in with themselves and share something like, "I feel that too," as they walk over for a hug, "I don't have time in this moment to connect beyond this, but let's find some time later tonight or tomorrow." Sharing with description in the present moment without a larger, six-steps-down-the-road expectation creates more connection and intimacy.

Step 4: Share in Digestible Pieces

I know it's tempting to launch into a Hamlet-style monologue about how you are feeling. You and your partner are finally talking about sex! You have a backlog that is charging forward, and you want to be heard. You also may be externally processing things to find the right language as you discover how you feel and what you want. Yet, I imagine that you actually want your partner to hear you, understand you, and receive you. Human attention can only focus for so long before needing a break to digest. This is especially true with sensation and defense-packed topics like sexuality. So, instead of getting it all out at once, slow down and share just a couple of sentences or one idea with a breath at the end. Allow your partner time to listen, reflect, share what they heard you say, and ask if they heard you right.

While communicating feelings and experiences in an embodied way, it is important to make sure that you and your partner are feeling present and connected. This is a different way to communicate than you do on a daily, more mundane basis, where we end up rattling off a bunch of details or a story from the day. Embodied communication asks us to forgo the Hamlet monologue that speaks volumes to no one in particular and instead speak in digestible pieces directly to an intimate partner so that they have time to receive what you are saying and track how their body is responding to you.

Step 5: Honor Your Partner's Experience With Gratitudes

Embodied communication is a powerful and also vulnerable way to communicate. You may find that you begin to feel closer to your partner as you share with each other the experience of your inner landscape. You may also find that you feel uncomfortable and activated by what they say. Regardless of the scenario, make sure that you begin by offering them a gratitude such as *thank you for sharing that with me*. Offering an appreciation for sharing inner feelings sends the message that your relationship is safe enough to be honest and that, even if something difficult is shared, it will most likely produce a favorable response.

Gratitude and appreciation are key to successful dialogue with an intimate partner. Beginning in the 1970s, clinical psychologist John Gottman and Silver (2015) studied couples and learned that the more positive affirmations and appreciations that a couple expressed, especially during arguments, the more likely they were to rate their relationship positively and stay together over the years. A genuine appreciation for something, even when you disagree, goes a very long way.

Connect With the Emotional Body First and Then Problem-Solve

Emotions have an intelligence that we can learn to understand and connect with as a way of engaging in intimacy with a partner. Emotions are a collection of bodily sensations, facial expressions, and movement qualities that coalesce into an overall feeling. We share common emotions with every other human on the planet, but the context in which we feel them and how we deal with them differ based on culture, family, and individual experiences.

There is a physiological difference between being primarily in *emotion brain* and being in *problem-solving brain.* This is a very simplified way of saying that when emotions are activated to the point that the nervous system is dysregulated, the most brain often activates one of two strategies to deal with the dysregulation. Atkinson (2005) refers to this as a core difference of problem-solving first versus understanding first as methods to resolve upset feelings in a relationship, and people tend to trend toward one or the other as a strategy. When in emotion brain, the primary activity is in the limbic and hind brain—the emotional and the primal instinctual areas of the brain, respectively—and the frontal lobes may have less activity. Problem-solving brain, on the other hand, is when the whole brain is active—the instinctual, the emotional, and the frontal lobes of the brain—or when someone has bypassed the emotion brain altogether to function from the frontal lobes as a coping mechanism to avoid emotional discomfort. The front of the brain, or the prefrontal cortex, is where complex thinking, impulse control, and planning happen. Instinct and emotion support problem-solving when the nervous system is mostly regulated. Neither way is right or wrong, just different. But this can feel like a problem when you and your partner have different strategies.

When your intimate partner is struggling emotionally in the moment, offering them advice won't work, not because they don't want to try, but because their physiology simply doesn't have the capability.

I encourage my couples to first meet their partner's emotions, reflecting what they see and hear them saying (*it sounds like you are feeling really sad about what happened*) and letting them know what makes sense about their sadness based on what you know about them (it makes sense that you feel sad. *I know that it was really important to you that that situation worked out.*) You can also share how it feels to see them in this emotional state (*my heart hurts to see you sad like this*). This also helps the problem-solving-brain-oriented partner to slow down and tune into their own emotions—how they might be impacted by their partner's emotions and refine their ability to identify and work with their emotions. When both people are tuning into their emotions together, this supports relational intimate attunement.

Once you have contacted your partner emotionally, *then* you can ask if they want to talk about any problem-solving in the situation, which could include simply going for a walk together—moving the body helps move emotions so they can be released to regulate the nervous system and experience relief.

When you are speaking about sexual intimacy and one of you feels frustrated or upset, the other partner, contacting their partner's emotion brain state, can say something like, "it makes sense that you are feeling frustrated with this aspect of our sex life" (having different desires, not having time for intimacy, having low libido, not enjoying how sex is initiated, etc.). "I am here to work on this with you together. Let me know when you are open to reading the intimacy book that we just bought together." Especially when it comes to sexual intimacy, supporting each other to feel safe enough to be close helps to calm the primal threat response that can surface in the nervous system so that you can continue to be open to each other.

Once you both are more regulated and within your window of capacity, you can begin the embodied communication practice.

3

SEXUAL WIRING IN RELATIONSHIPS

How Nervous System States Impact Your Arousal Anatomy

Your arousal anatomy is a wise organ system of the body. Not only does it have the potential for immense pleasure and transformative connection with a partner, but it also gives you important information about what you need to feel safe enough to drop into a pleasure experience. It is also an important indicator of your overall health and well-being. As we've discussed previously, this organ system is also deeply interconnected with your nervous system and therefore is an indicator of whether you are calm and relaxed, excited and energetic, or stressed and shut down. In essence, your arousal anatomy has the potential to be an important internal resource for you and for your relationship.

When challenges arise with arousal anatomy, I often hear people become exasperated or feel that their body has failed or betrayed them. Many people experience a kind of body dysmorphia with their arousal anatomy—it is difficult to enjoy or trust areas of the body that you may have been told to fear, laugh at, avoid, and suppress. At times, these sociocultural messages are meant to protect, other times to control, yet are pervasive because many cultures find it extraordinarily uncomfortable to speak about the arousal anatomy. This creates a distorted lens through which this tender and expressive part of the body is felt experientially and visibly seen. Instead of embracing arousal anatomy as a wise indicator of wellness and a source of pleasure, we often inadvertently approach it with judgment, criticism, and fear. This creates confusion and overwhelm, so the nervous system activates body armor against this uncomfortable experience, resulting in disconnection and an unconscious relationship with arousal anatomy.

When arousal anatomy becomes an unconscious area of the body, adverse reactions begin to happen. The vast potential for pleasure and connection is

DOI: 10.4324/9781003508984-5

neglected, and the ability to modulate arousal is diminished; therefore, it can be difficult to amplify arousal when you want to—and boundary violations are more likely to occur when arousal is not contained. Early signs of illness or infection are missed, which makes it difficult to advocate for care. Intimate partners experience disconnection due to misunderstanding, insensitivity, or different sets of values related to the body, and the opportunity for problem-solving and deep healing is missed when medical conditions impact sexual function, but it is uncomfortable to speak to care providers about sexual symptoms.

But what if the challenges that arise are your arousal anatomy speaking important information to you, giving you direct clues and information that you need to make good decisions about your body? What if you turned to your arousal anatomy as a friend, as you embrace their difficulty, offer them comfort, and discover how to inspire them to awaken their potential? The truth is that the variability of arousal anatomy is normal. Challenges that arise are opportunities to learn more about yourself and your body, and arousal anatomy can rewire itself after physical, emotional, or medical trauma.

Let's explore the different ways that you can learn to relate with your arousal anatomy and develop meaningful language and bodyful practices that you can share with a partner.

What Is Arousal Anatomy?

Arousal anatomy is the elegant network of sensitive, nerve-filled tissue that runs through the body. I see this wise organ system as being made up of two general categories that are intricately linked: the central and the peripheral arousal anatomy systems.

The *Central Arousal Anatomy System* is what you would normally identify as the more obvious erogenous zones found in the midline of the body: lips, genitals, breasts/chest, and anal area. The central system contains erectile tissue and the densely enervated tissue of the genitals and nipples. This is the focus of most sex education teaching, as they are more directly related to reproduction and therefore the focus of the strictest regulation. The most common definition of sex—penetrative sex or genital-to-genital contact—directly involves the central arousal anatomy. It often gets the most direct attention during sex and generally is the first area of the body to be touched when people are in a *spontaneous desire* state (spontaneously aroused), when engaging in a "quickie," or when attempting to get pregnant.

Touch and the central arousal anatomy system can often feel confusing for people in intimate relationships—specifically, identifying what kind of contact feels good, for how long, and in what circumstances. As you explore your anatomy with yourself and with your partner, remember that touch that feels good when you are fully in the altered state of arousal doesn't necessarily feel good when you are not aroused. So, slow down when you explore, enter the practice of embodied consent, and don't jump to immediate assumptions about what is enjoyable or not.

You may notice that there are times when the pace of your arousal anatomy doesn't align with your intimate partner. This is a normal result of your nervous system coming from different places and moving at different speeds or rhythms. Perhaps one of you is in more of a spontaneous desire state, turned on and already being picked up by the *momentum of arousal—the pace at which the momentum of arousal builds toward more intense and altered state peak moments, fueled by oxytocin and vassopressin*—while the other is in a more responsive state and still decelerating a busy mind into a place of relaxation so that they can access pleasure in the first place (Porges, 2011). I encourage you not to always move at the pace of the partner with the faster momentum if you feel dysregulated—pushing a nervous system to move faster rarely works. No one likes to be hurried, especially when enjoyment is the goal. Instead, move at the pace of connection with yourselves and with each other. Practicing embodied consent helps the partner with the distracted or slower-to-arouse nervous system to listen to their body, determine what their body needs to soften, and then rise into pleasure. Then they can invite their partner to join them in what feels good.

Moving at the pace of connection and supporting the partner with a slower arousal momentum is also helpful in having safer sex that supports the health and wellness of the body. For example, having penetrative sex before the erectile tissue of the vulva is fully aroused and engorged with blood increases the chance of infections. When heightened arousal causes the erectile tissue around the urethra to fill with blood, it squeezes the urethra shut so bacteria are less likely to enter. Without full arousal and engorgement, the urethra is more open and therefore more vulnerable to infection.

Central arousal anatomy benefits from calling on the whole body for support. This is where it is useful to turn to your peripheral arousal anatomy system for clues about what is needed for a pleasurable experience.

The *Peripheral Arousal Anatomy System* is the rest of your body. Yes, your whole body has the potential for pleasure and arousal! While the peripheral areas are often relegated to foreplay and often don't "count" for sexual play in mainstream dialogue, the whole body can be engaged to be a source of pleasure and also amplify a pleasurable sensory experience in connection with the central arousal anatomy. With the support of breath and movement, the sensation of pleasure can be dispersed and broadened throughout the central and peripheral arousal anatomy.

The peripheral arousal anatomy can also be called on to modulate the arousal of the central arousal anatomy. If you feel you are becoming highly aroused more quickly than your partner, you can breathe into your peripheral arousal anatomy to redirect pleasurable energy and delay orgasm without shutting down. Those in a *responsive desire* state (aroused through intentional touch and sensual connection) benefit from attention to their peripheral system first to awaken their central system if that is what is desired. So, if your central arousal anatomy response is muted, breath and movement from your periphery can direct more pleasurable sensations toward your erectile tissue. When the nervous system is relaxed-excited, warm, and interested in connection, you often detect this first through your peripheral system.

Pleasure is accessible in both the central and peripheral arousal anatomy systems in both sexual and non-sexual situations. Let's look at pleasure more broadly. Your somatic self is a source of pleasure in daily, non-sexual experiences, such as while exercising, engaging in a hobby, eating, getting a massage, swaying back and forth in a regular rhythm, or while resting. In fact, the more the peripheral arousal anatomy is engaged in daily pleasurable practices that are not of a directly sexual nature, the more capacity your body will develop for intimacy, overall health, and a sense of well-being.

Take a moment to consider daily practices and activities that feel good to you and list them. You could list your daily yoga or workout time, your morning tea, massage trade with a partner, dancing, eating a delicious meal, listening to music, meditation, and so on. As long as it is a nourishing, consensual, and intentional activity, it counts. When you are engaging in these activities, notice how you feel in your body: where are the places that feel good, and what are the sensations that you notice which indicate that you are enjoying the experience, and where are those sensations located? What are the movement qualities that generate a feeling of pleasure? Pleasure can present itself in many forms, so pay attention to when pleasure feels intense and exciting, warm and swaying, tingling and relaxing, and so on. This is the beginning of your somatic exploration of your arousal anatomy.

Getting to know the movement qualities of your peripheral *and* central arousal anatomy will support you in learning what it needs to become excited and expand into the space. Movement qualities and sensations are the native language of the body, and they speak the truth of what is happening and where to begin the process of support and sequencing of movement in order to unwind the challenge of the moment or rewire habitual patterns of retraction.

The arousal anatomy systems are designed to grow in feel-good situations—specifically, arousal anatomy has the capacity to *expand*. Remember how a body that feels safe enough takes up more space? It is true for central arousal anatomy as well! Erectile tissue expands when it is filled with blood and softens when the height of arousal has passed. Muscles and connective tissues expand when a full in-breath is taken, and they soften when a full-out breath is released. In somatic dance/movement therapy terms, we describe a sensation and movement quality of *widening* when this expansion takes place and *narrowing* when followed by the release.

It is important to note that a body that widens into the space and releases or softens as it narrows is a body that feels safe enough to take up space and then relax. Arousal anatomy follows the same principles of widening and narrowing—safe enough to expand and safe enough to surrender to the release in a gesture of active yield. Central arousal anatomy that does not feel safe or interested in the present moment contact is more likely to contract, make itself smaller, sometimes to the point of causing discomfort or pain. This is true of genitals as well as of the muscles and tissues of the pelvic bowl, which can contract under stress—this is your somatic system telling you that the body is currently under duress and needs support.

Arousal non-concordance is an experience where part of your central and/or peripheral arousal anatomy is expanding, while another part is contracting instead of widening or releasing. In other words, part of you feels turned on and interested in connection, while another part of you does not. When we turn to your arousal anatomy as a wise organ system of the body and practice somatic listening, we can get curious about what the contracted part is telling us. Ask the contracted part of your body directly, *What doesn't feel safe or interesting? What does it need to soften without force?* We'll discuss arousal non-concordance in-depth in the next chapter, but for now, remember that both the central and peripheral arousal anatomy systems evolve over time in terms of what feels good and how they respond to sensual engagement. Allow yourself to be surprised by what you discover! While the responsiveness of your arousal anatomy systems is an interplay of biology and early experiences, new learning can occur and broaden your repertoire.

Forming a Healthy Relationship With Arousal Anatomy

Take a moment to ask yourself, after reading more about arousal anatomy, what is your relationship with your arousal anatomy like? Do you find that you avoid these areas of your body, or do you connect with them as a source of pleasure and information? How would you describe your relationship with your partner's arousal anatomy?

Your relationship with your arousal anatomy says a lot about your relationship to pleasure in general. And the more comfort and familiarity that you have with your own body, the more you can connect with yourself and an intimate partner in a pleasurable and meaningful way that enriches your connection.

It can be tempting to go along with the perceived standards of how arousal anatomy should look or behave. These standards are primarily assumptions that have been developed through minimal research and are heavily influenced by biased sociocultural standards of sex. Consider that, beneath all the assumptions that you may have about your arousal anatomy from the years of living in a paradoxically sex-averse and sex-sensationalizing culture, there is the true body story that you carry. This story tells about how your body was impacted by the environment that you grew up in, from your family, to friends, to media, and it tells you about how your habits and rhythms as a couple encourage expression or suppression. This is why it is important to practice *secure attachment* with your own body and arousal anatomy. Between the sociocultural misinformation about sexuality, the external labeling of your body experience, and the myriad of body transformations that we experience throughout our lives, we need a way of being in relationship with our bodies that is life-giving, not life-draining, and makes room to embrace change.

As you and a partner dive into the embodied story of arousal anatomy, you will be better able to connect with each other—to the degree that you can connect with and self-reflect from the genuine, present-moment experience of your body. You can learn to work *with* your arousal anatomy and nervous system states in a realistic and personally meaningful way.

To form a healthy connection with the body, I guide my clients in developing a *secure attachment* with their body and arousal anatomy. While we usually talk about establishing a secure attachment within the context of relationships, it can be applied to your relationship with your body to spectacular effect. This then creates a lens and a set of habits that you can apply to the body of your partner.

In the field of relationship therapy, *secure relationship attachment* (Levine & Heller, 2010; Fern et.al., 2020) is elevated as a healthy way of relating with the important people in your life. This is the kind of relationship where you feel supported and received with love, embracing moments of flow together while making space for the difficulties that arise in the relationship without blaming or rejection. You feel you can go out into the world and return to this person feeling welcomed and feeling their interest in how you are and what you experienced. You and your partner often feel emotionally regulated in each other's presence, even though you still have challenges from time to time. It is normal to feel disappointment or frustration in intimate connection, and when secure attachment is present, you can turn these moments into learning experiences that deepen emotional intimacy and self-awareness.

A secure attachment with your arousal anatomy can look like prioritizing listening to what your arousal anatomy is experiencing alongside the rest of your body—instead of othering your arousal anatomy, it is treated as an integral part of the whole of your somatic self. While you may feel frustrated when you get an infection or are not getting aroused during sexual intimacy, you slow down to listen to what your arousal anatomy needs to feel better, to soften, to get turned on. You advocate for your arousal anatomy with your intimate partner during intimacy or with your medical doctor when it is impacted by medications or surgery. You know to check with your peripheral arousal anatomy to support your arousal anatomy. You also prioritize touching your own body with kindness and engage in activities that are pleasurable (and always consensual) on a regular basis.

This is very different from the other relationship attachment types, such as anxious, avoidant, or ambivalent attachment. Anxious/avoidant relationship dynamics feel more like a tense or rigid clinging to expectations and assumptions. You feel constricted or exasperated much of the time, and that easeful way of relating is hard to find. When disappointment or hurt feelings happen, it is hard to let it go and shift back into vulnerability, connection, and learning. Meanwhile, ambivalent attachment can feel like a desire to be both close and back away at the same time, often causing a freeze or flight response.

While secure attachment can seem difficult to achieve when it comes to sexuality, it can be learned and applied to both your intimate connection with your partner and your connection with your own body.

At its essence, secure attachment is a sequence or series of steps, a bodyful practice that can be created and repeated. It is a practice that encourages moments for breath and movement, for rupture and repair, and a welcoming back into connection without agenda, but with intentions for awareness, openness to learning, understanding, and trying something new. Let's use the example of sexual intimacy with a partner to demonstrate a bodyful practice of secure attachment (notice the underlying foundation of embodied consent):

- *Action*: You are beginning intimacy with your partner, and they reach for your central arousal anatomy right away.
- *Awareness—check in with your body*: You notice your pelvic floor tighten and your body subtly retract from your partner's touch. Your tight pelvic floor tells you that the touch was too sudden.
- *Validate your body:* Tell your body, "that makes sense that it felt too fast." You recognize that you are not feeling attuned with your partner, and they are not attuned with you. What is your context? Did you have a stressful day, or is the room too cold? Yes, it's time to slow down.
- *Advocate for your body*: Tell your partner you would like to slow down and tell them what you notice.

> *I notice that my pelvic floor is feeling tight and not ready for contact. I think it would feel good to begin with a shower or holding each other so that my peripheral nervous system can relax and see if my central arousal anatomy comes online.*

- *Shift activity*: Begin with the activity that feels most interesting (shower or holding) and then ask, "what do I notice now?" "What is feeling good?"
- *Check in again and share what your body notices now*: Share with your partner what you are enjoying and invite central arousal anatomy contact when you feel ready.

Extend this secure attachment to your partner. Open your learning-mind to recognize the beauty and challenges of your partner and their unique body story, broadening understanding and deepening your shared connection. This leads to evolution of your intimate life as you increase awareness of your whole body connection and honor each other's body autonomy and body stories.

Practicing secure attachment with yourself and your partner in the intimate realm gives you space to regulate your nervous system—to transition from the Sexual Inhibition System (SIS) to the SES that we discussed in Chapter 1. Remember that the SES is online when you feel relaxed, interested, and open for connection. The sensation can feel like a widening of the inner somatic landscape. This sense of widening and fullness extends to your arousal anatomy. The SES allows blood and oxygen to flow more freely throughout the whole body, expanding erectile and other soft tissues of the body, and heightening pleasurable sensations. In addition, your mind probably feels more relaxed and present in the moment, allowing you to connect more with your embodied experience and your intimate partner in a meaningful way.

When the SIS is active when more of an anxious-avoidant or ambivalent dynamic is present, the muscles are more constricted, and the midline of the body can feel tight and also uncomfortably shaky. This extends to your arousal anatomy. Because blood and oxygen are not flowing freely, your central arousal anatomy feels tight, numb, or painful. Erectile tissue is less likely to engorge with blood or lubricate, and orgasm feels elusive or happens quicker than you want. When in your SIS, your mind is probably distracted or narrowly fixating on something stressful or critical, preventing you from feeling pleasure or connecting with your partner.

The SIS can activate even within a securely attached relationship with yourself and with your partner. Everyone has a body story that includes challenges, old wounds, and body changes that can be distressing. The point here is not to avoid being in your SIS—the point is to identify when you are in your SIS, to slow down with the practice of *embodied consent*, and ask the places in your body that feel discomfort what they need to soften back into the present moment and reignite excitement.

Invite your arousal anatomy back into a place of curiosity, giving yourself permission to follow your satisfaction cycle (Bainbridge Cohen, 2012) as you actively yield into your body, and then mobilize (push) your movement and awareness together to reach and grasp what feels pleasurable to you, pulling it (the sensation, your partner) toward you so that you can again yield and rest into enjoyment and exploration. Due to our socialization, we often learn to de-prioritize exploration of what is interesting to us with full-body participation, instead grabbing onto pleasure in disembodied ways as we get stuck in the reach and grasp part of the sequence, never fully yielding into the nourishment of pleasure. With this full sequence, you can learn how to relate to your body challenges in a way that supports learning and adaptation.

Engaging the satisfaction cycle with embodied consent is an important component of secure attachment. When arousal anatomy has built up body armor to protect itself (tightening of the vaginal canal, difficulty with erection, orgasming quicker than you want, etc.), your body needs compassion and space to explore what the body armor is trying to do for you. The protective response will not respond well to force; it will only amplify the body armor. Instead, engage in the embodied consent practice to support, uncover an underlying need, and find that relaxed state of yield that allows for receptivity of genuine pleasure.

Learning About Arousal Anatomy Is a Meaningful Process

You get to decide together what is *meaningful* about the places where you flow together; decide what is *meaningful* about your challenges; what is *meaningful* about when your sexual intimacy lines up, as well as when it hits a snag and needs to adapt. Mis-attunement interrupting attunement is normal and can be an opportunity to experience the rhythm of tension and release, which, when we feel safe enough, can build tone and flexibility into the relational dance. Even with body challenges, arousal anatomy can rewire itself and adapt to new conditions of life events, when you create an intimate space together that is curious and full of breath and movement. I find that when we have a sense of purpose as a guiding star with an effective set of skills, navigating difficult terrain becomes doable.

So, let's talk about some skills and practices to help you conduct your own somatic research together. Let the connection between your arousal anatomy and nervous system states be the central subject, instead of trying to get your arousal anatomy to behave the way you want or expect.

What Ignites Your Arousal?

As you are exploring your arousal anatomy as a wise organ system, begin to notice—what are your intrinsic arousal igniters and extrinsic arousal igniters? Intrinsic arousal igniters are things within yourself that activate arousal, such as fantasy and visualization, feeling the pleasure of movement, and anything that generates pleasure from the inside out. Extrinsic arousal igniters are things outside of your body that activate an arousal and pleasure response within you, such as seeing your partner undress or express desire for you, watching a sexy movie, or listening to sensual music (you get to define what is sexy or sensual to you).

Let's use both of these sources in the next exercise to help you get to know your arousal systems and deepen your relationship with your arousal anatomy.

Explore Your Arousal Anatomy from the Inside Out—Identify an activity that you love to do. This could be something non-sexual, like dancing or cooking, or it could be something sexual, like receiving or offering an erotic massage. Notice the sensations that arise from within your inner landscape (texture, temperature, shape, movement quality). Notice the movement impulse from the sensation (warmth is a widening and softening movement impulse, and tingling is a variable soft prickling movement impulse). Allow the inner movement to move you, your hands, spine, and hips. Sequence the movement directly from the origin point of sensation out through your end points—hands and feet, crown of the head, and tailbone. Describe the sensations to yourself as you follow the movement. Then, share with your partner. Identify three sensations and/or movement qualities as you clarify your movement and say *my sexuality is . . .* and then list the sensations. Partner, thank them for sharing! Then share your own.

Notice how it feels to connect this experience of pleasure, even in a non-sexual context, to your overall sexuality. Pleasure *is* accessible to you, even in the everyday activities that you discover or prioritize.

Connect with your own somatic landscape. Find a home in your pleasure. For yourself. By yourself. With your partner. The more you cultivate your body as home, the better your experience of your relationship and partner sex will be.

4

INTRODUCING THE WHOLE-PERSON SEXUAL RESPONSE CYCLE IN RELATIONSHIP

How do you shift from the day-to-day mundane tasks of life to the altered-state flow of attuned intimacy and sexual arousal with a partner? For many, this feels like a big leap, especially in the years after settling into a committed partnership. When you can no longer rely on the endorphins of a new connection, it can feel quite frustrating and confusing when your attraction and love for each other do not quickly transition into arousal and desire for sex.

When the flow into arousal feels easier, you probably don't slow down to notice what got you there—it may have felt totally spontaneous, totally *natural*. You may not have paid any attention to how the environment, your nervous system state, how you were relating to yourself, your stress level, and how the quality of connection between you and your partner supported the building of pleasure and arousal in your bodies. Yet, all these circumstances directly affect whether or not you can get turned on, focus on the present moment, build arousal toward peak moments of pleasure, and feel delightfully connected afterward.

However inconvenient, life circumstances and a committed relationship structure change your access to your sexual interests. How can this be? Often, the reason is tied to investing your mutual energy in other priorities such as managing household duties and finances, getting pregnant and raising kids, or establishing and maintaining careers. People often let their sex life drift, thinking it will naturally get better once the house is bought, once their child is a few years old, or once they are established in their careers, until a real disconnect becomes a glaring drag on their connection. It may be surprising, but you don't have a *sexual energy reserve tank* apart from your main energy tank—your total energy comes from the same place,

DOI: 10.4324/9781003508984-6

and when you invest in the tasks of commitment and establishing a life together, you may not have the energy left to invest in the activities and the relationship structure that nurtures a vivacious sexual relationship. When intelligent sexuality is not already baked into these life processes related to commitment, it can feel as if you've simply lost that kind of connection with each other—you have grown apart, you are older, you don't have time—and reclaiming a conscious connection may feel overwhelming. As my mentor, somatic psychotherapist Dr. Christine Caldwell says, *consciousness is expensive, metabolically.* You probably sense this. You intuitively know that learning about the expressiveness of arousal anatomy and what it needs within a committed intimate partnership can take energy, and accessing the awake and aware qualities of consciousness may feel daunting. Where do you start? How do you find the time? I often hear clients say that their schedule gets in the way of practicing their new skills. Consciousness is necessary to learn the information and skills to optimize your sex life. And with the right map and guidance on how to incorporate it into your day-to-day interactions, it is absolutely possible.

Fortunately, sexual responsiveness is not a mysterious process that you either have or don't have with your partner. You are already doing things every day that can be an effective domain to study your sexuality together. (I'll circle back to this soon.)

As a sex and relationship therapist, a couple's unique dynamic related to the sexual responsiveness of their bodies begins with exploring where their sexuality is alive and well and where the challenges exist. I begin by asking a series of questions to assess the couple's perception of the challenge:

- At what point before, during, or after sex do you begin to feel disconnected from your partner?
- At what point before, during, or after sex do you lose track of yourself?
- What used to feel great that now feels unsatisfying?
- At what point before, during, or after sex do you find that you are more in your head than in your body?
- Do you find that you avoid sexual connection? Or do you find yourself dropping into the same habits of sex—the same location, same order of activities, or same fantasies?
- Do you find that you avoid affection? Or do you only initiate touch with some form of sex in mind? Or, do you only initiate touch from a nonsexual place with your intimate partner?

Through these questions, I can begin to understand the roots of the challenge. We can quickly begin to narrow down the stage of intimacy where the disconnect happens and learn the most likely context when it happens. Then I can ask more detailed questions: is it about touch, how sex is being initiated, and how their arousal anatomy fits together, their mismatched pace or rhythm, or their lack of time together to feel their connection?

The most obvious challenges that people identify as sexual challenges are how sex is initiated, arguments related to whether or not someone is *in the mood,* whether or not the partners can orgasm or if someone orgasms before they want to, or uncomfortable feelings and disconnection after the heightened arousal of sex has passed. Sex, however, is a multifaceted dance where both partners play a part, and the challenge does not start at the moment that you think—it's probably been simmering for a while. When challenges arise, this realm benefits from focusing not just on the challenge itself but also on the surrounding context and circumstances that create the challenge in the first place and that continue to create a pattern of disconnect and difficulty over time. Just like a knot in a muscle, the knot didn't come first—the body organization of tension and lack of structural integrity came first.

As we explore how the whole relationship is organized and how their intimacy fits in, I often find that people have very little verbal ability to describe their sex life, let alone put words to what feels great and what feels challenging, because where would you have learned this language? Middle school sex education? Nope. At your urologist's or gynecologist's office? Probably not. One of the core facets of my work with couples is helping them build accurate, meaningful language and an interactive map for their sexual response during intimacy. This begins with defining sex for yourselves.

Define Your Own Sexy-Time

The first concept that I introduce is the concept of *sexy-time*—a space for sexual intimacy that is defined by you, the intimate partners, to be personally meaningful, emphasizing that intimacy is about pleasure and connection, not ideals and expectations. This is intended to free you from the constraints of the word *sex,* which is so heavily typecast and often limited to the dominant-culture definition. Sexy-time gives you a vision for what is possible in your intimate connection and expression of pleasurable life energy.

Take a few moments here to find the language that best describes the qualities of this realm for your connection. Let's explore how to find language that is descriptive, personally relevant, and inspiring.

Take three full breaths in with three long breaths out and settle your body into your seat. Visualize your best sexually intimate experience with each other (remember that time in the hotel after the symphony?) or your favorite non-sexual physical experience with each other (remember that time hiking or playing pickleball?) Let this memory fill your mind and body. Visualize the weather, sun on your skin, a breeze or rain, a warm room with soft light, and so on. Visualize the aesthetics of the space: lush with trees and water, music and comfortable seats, and so on. Visualize the arch of time, the events and interactions, the conversations, the glances at each other, and the progression of pleasurable qualities of touch. Let your body feel this memory in vivid detail.

Now, notice what happens in your somatic self. Let your awareness be like a bird flying over your internal landscape, hovering over the landmarks of sensation. Breathe around the sensations that you find, allowing them to expand and become brighter. Describe these sensations to yourself as descriptively as possible; notice temperature, texture, size and shape, and movement quality. Every sensation has a movement quality to it, so notice the rhythm, pace, and directional quality of the sensation. Full breath in, long breath out. Right from the origin point of sensation, allow your body to physically express this movement quality. Let it sequence, inch by inch from the beginning all the way out to your endpoints (hands and feet, crown of the head, and tail bone). Repeat the movement as you clarify, slowing down as the movement traverses a place in your body that feels stuck (a tight muscle and a joint that gets stuck) and, instead of forcing the movement, allow your body to slowly find a way around the stuck place, like water around rock. Allow yourself to be curious and surprised about where the movement takes you.

Write a few words down in your journal to describe the sensations in your body and their movement qualities. This is your body speaking to you about how this pleasurable experience lives in your body.

Choose three words and a movement quality to share with your partner. You can say, "our sexy-time is . . ." and say the three words while expressing the movement. For example, you may have felt lightness in your chest and a warm, expanding sensation across your shoulders. You found yourself elongating your spine and opening your arms to your sides. Share with your partner: "our sexy-time is lightness and warmth expanding." Thank your partner for sharing with you and reflect out loud to them anything that you resonated with.

After both of you have shared, notice if your sensations and movement qualities align with or compliment each other. If one of you describes lightness and warmth expanding with arms slowly opening wide to your sides, your partner may express lifting, excited tension, and accelerating forward movement as they draw their hands up the center of the body. These movement phrases are different yet compatible. Share your movements simultaneously to notice how you may fit together. If it feels like it doesn't fit together clearly, engage your breath to support your movement, and try slowing down and initiating your movements at different times. Get curious about the place of alignment.

This is now your vision of what is possible! Use it as an invitation to connect with each other. This is an *invitation,* not an *expectation.* Let your partner know when you feel interested in some light, warm, expansive time together. Remember that the body needs a period of transition and build up to and arrive at the heightened arousal and pleasure space, so once you establish the qualities intended for your sexy-time space, you can deepen into learning *how* your body enters into that light, warm, and expansive place, which may allow you to then engage with consensual and pleasurable sexual responsiveness.

An Interactive Map for the Rhythm of Arousal Anatomy

Sexual responsiveness is a series or sequence of somatic and physiological sensations and expressions. As with any journey, a map is helpful to identify what your body needs to enter into the sexy-time space, identify the body expressions of sexual arousal, and understand the contextual factors that impact your sexual responsiveness with a partner. With this knowledge, you can have a shared language and a guide to help you focus on the relevant details and better navigate your sexual dynamic. Instead of looking for a model for *functional sex*—which could be anything from maintenance sex (the kind of sex that you have because you are checking a box on the to-do list) to fulfilling, intimate sex that honors your unique styles—the *Whole-Person Sexual Response* map that I present here makes space for your actual, lived experience, unique qualities, and all. It offers a framework for evaluating and working with the rhythms of your arousal anatomy during sex without shaming anyone for not fitting with some irrelevant norm.

This map is not static. It does not hold you to a certain normative standard regardless of age and circumstance. Instead, it has the ability to flex and change and breathe along with you as your body and life factors change over time.

This section presents the model in stages of how your body responds to sexual intimacy and how to support yourself and each other throughout the progression of sexual arousal. These stages do not necessarily happen in the order that they are presented here—you may find that you begin at a different stage in different contexts—but they are presented in this order for clarity and for ease in you doing your own reconnaissance within your intimate relationship.

Remember that the way you embody these stages is heavily dependent on your unique body with your unique collection of life experiences and physiological circumstances. How you respond within the progression of sexual arousal now may be different from how you responded when you were younger and will be different from how you may respond in the future as you age and experience body changes and different life circumstances. Various physical factors can affect these stages (refer to Chapter 6 on sexuality challenges), and relationship difficulties can cause you to conflate emotional disconnection and wounding with sexual challenges (see Chapters 1 and 2 on embodied consent and communication). Discerning the sources of your challenges within your sexual responsiveness—the roots of why it is difficult to experience arousal, desire, or the peak moment of orgasm—is the part of your relationship story that contains the fuel for your evolution as intimate partners. Deeply meaningful relationships are not formed on the foundation of ease—they are forged within a shared purpose, meaningful shared struggle, and mutual personal growth as you compassionately explore challenges together.

Let's explore the map.

Origin of the Human Sexual Response Model

Between 1957 and 1965, researchers William Masters, a gynecologist, and Virginia Johnson, a psychologist, developed their model of the *human sexual response* (HSR) (Masters & Johnson, 1966) through their research study observing 382 women and 312 men in coitus. Their important research, despite controversy from a conservative social culture, gifted us with a direct look at the responsiveness of arousal anatomy and overall physiology of sexual stimulation. Their research presented sex as a natural and normal activity that is beneficial outside of its reproductive function.

This valuable four-stage model—excitement, plateau, orgasm, and resolution—supports an understanding of the potential of your body's response to sexual stimulation. It has become the basis of the sexual function disorders diagnosed by doctors and therapists around the world. However, this model does not allow for variability of experience or information on how and what supports you to shift from an unaroused state into an aroused and orgasmic state. It also doesn't place value on peak moments of pleasure not identified as genital orgasm. Unfortunately, because of the nature of their research and the ethical limits on using human subjects in research, Masters and Johnson (or any other researchers) were not able to replicate their study with a population other than the majority of white, highly educated, heteronormative, able-bodied, highly orgasmic couples who participated in their original study (Roach, 2008).

The limitations of the HSR model, however, do not have to be left to run the show. Other sex researchers, educators, and therapists have broadened the applicability of this map by adding the concept of *desire* in a triphasic model of desire–excitement–orgasm (Kaplan, 1995), by identifying the non-linear trajectory responsive desire seen more often in women in long-term relationships (Basson, 2000), and recognizing sexual response relies on a dual-control system in the nervous system of *accelerators or inciters* and *brakes or suppressors* (Bankroft and Jansen, 2009; Kaplan, 1995). When combined with a somatic perspective that takes into account the whole, evolving person as a member of an intimate attachment within the changing context of life, we can increase its applicability and inclusivity.

Let's explore the six stages of a whole-person sexual response approach that you can use as an interactive map with your partner to learn the landscape of your sexual dynamic that incorporates your individual style and nervous system strategies.

SECTION 2

Navigating Sexuality Challenges Together

5

THE SIX STAGES OF THE WHOLE-PERSON SEXUAL RESPONSE CYCLE

In my first book, *Whole-Body Sex,* I introduced the *Whole-Person Sexual Response Cycle:* a cyclical map that combines a somatic perspective with the traditional sexual response cycle (see Figure 5.1). This model follows the somatic rhythm of movement of generative energy through the body, and it can help you identify what gets your life energy moving and surging. While the first book focused on an individual's experience, here I will illustrate how to use the map to support your combined experience.

As you study this responsiveness in you and a partner, remember that this sequence does not unfold flawlessly—it is often marked by pauses, interruptions, and a distracted mind. This normal variability requires that you take an out-breath, refocus your attention on your inner experience, practice embodied consent, and find attunement again as you assist your body to return to the pleasure of the present moment.

Couples often find themselves expressing judgments about themselves or a partner related to the normal variability of sexual responsiveness. In the absence of good sex education, pop culture inserts its fantasy and its jokes around the challenges of partner sex, coloring our perspective with unrealistic expectations—a ridiculous depiction of a realm central to intimate life. Breathe in compassion and some grace for yourself and your partner as you begin to explore together.

I encourage you to begin exploring how your energy may follow this map in non-sexual situations first. Our generative, creative energy moves through us in many ways and in many different contexts, so allow yourselves to be inclusive of your experience in response to *any* pleasurable activity that generates the building/cresting/releasing rhythm of arousal energy, followed by a life-affirming integration. This map knows that sex is not your only avenue

DOI: 10.4324/9781003508984-8

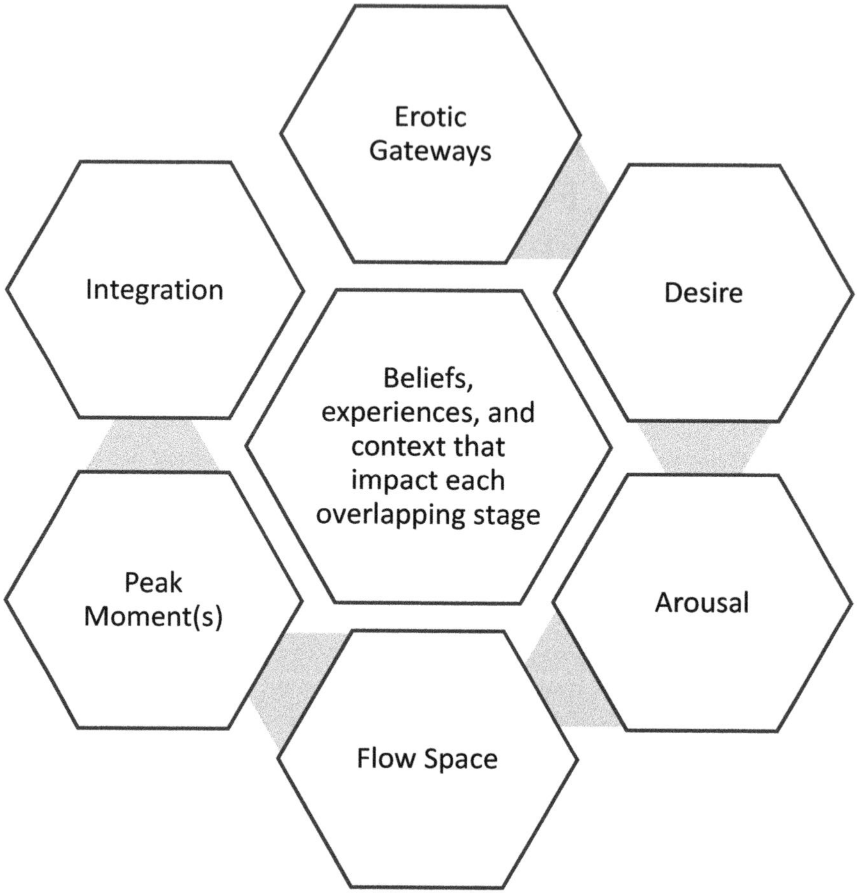

Figure 5.1 Whole Person Sexual Response Cycle.

for the kind of pleasure that volumizes your body and supports a whole-body connection to an intimate partner. By learning all the situations where your body experiences pleasure and connection—you don't necessarily have to include a bunch of new activities in your calendar—your daily life becomes more pleasurable, and this knowledge and fullness of bodily expression can be applied to the sexy-time space.

Stage 1: Erotic Gateways

Many of my clients talk about beginning sexual intimacy by cuddling, kissing, massaging, or just going straight for the central arousal anatomy. If you have a spontaneous desire style, this may be enough for you. However, this may not be enough for those with more of a responsive desire style, a high stress level, those caring for young children in the home, those who have experienced trauma, or people in long-term committed relationships who have settled into a place of auto-pilot or complacency with each other. Without engaging erotic gateways first, the "foreplay" type activities may not feel connective to generate arousal. Instead, you may find that you feel annoyed or distracted, internally fighting with yourself to just keep going or call off the lovemaking session altogether. This is one of those places where obligation and habitual patterns can rear their head—you just keep going thinking arousal will eventually kick in, you'll just get through it, or that your partner will eventually feel pleasure. Or you may be disconnected with your partner in a solo sex state during what is meant to be partner sex—but you leave the experience feeling confused and unsatisfied.

Erotic Gateways, the first stage of sexual responsiveness, are (1) what allows your body to relax enough to be receptive to pleasure and (2) what feels pleasurable enough to bring aliveness to the sensitive tissues and nerve pathways in the body. Erotic gateways begin to activate the release of pleasurable hormones and neurotransmitters in the endocrine and nervous systems, bringing balance to your nervous system state, which supports shifting from the social/sexual inhibition system (SIS) to the SES, allowing you to cultivate a sense of connection and attunement with your partner. As you engage in erotic gateways, the tightness or wall in your chest dissipates, your brow unfurrows, your stomach begins to soften and open, and a lightness awakens in your body—your spine lengthens, and your movement becomes less bound or rigid as it opens into a more fluid or energetic expression.

Think of erotic gateways as different-sized pebbles in a jar. There are the small daily pebbles, the medium-sized weekly or monthly pebbles, and the large once-a-year pebbles. Erotic gateways can be the following:

- Small pebble erotic gateways. These are the little things that bring you a daily moment of embodied pleasure, such as your morning tea and meditation, a hot shower, your daily bike ride or gym routine, the music that you play while driving or cooking dinner, and your evening porch hang time when the tasks of the day are done. These are the little practices that you are devoted to. *Take a moment to list the activities that are a part of your daily rituals, the things that lift you up on a regular basis. As you visualize each of these experiences, notice the sensations and movement qualities that awaken in the body and write them down in descriptive words (texture, temperature, size and shape, and movement qualities of pace, rhythm, volume, etc.).* In the bedroom (or wherever you have your sexy-time), this is the ambient music that you turn on, the temperature check in the room to make sure that it feels good, the comfortable and/or sexy clothing that you change into, and the audio erotica that turns you on and relaxes you while listening.

- Medium pebble erotic gateways. These are activities that you get to do once to a few times a week that take up a bit more time, such as your weekly date at the climbing gym, your game night or dance night with your friends, or dinner at that swanky bistro down the street. These are the activities that are immersive and transport you from the daily mundane. *Write down a few activities that you do separately and together that feel like mini weekly adventures or immersive experiences.* In the bedroom, medium pebble erotic gateways are when you have time for a sensual or erotic massage exchange, a sensory play adventure exploring different textures, temperatures, or pressure in the form of feathers, ice cubes, fringe, and so on, or time in the hot tub before sexy-time.
- Large pebble erotic gateways. These are the adventures that you get to do once to a few times a year—adventures that you tell stories about on the porch and feel the echo of excitement after the experience is over. This may be your annual camping trip, a yoga retreat, the island fly-fishing trip, a favorite holiday, or the night out on the town that feels like the most fun you have ever had. It's not just the experience that is the erotic gateway—the memory counts too. *Journal about a few substantial erotic gateways, the kind that you reminisce about with each other, and write down the descriptive somatic sensations and movement qualities that arise in you.* On a more overtly sexual note, this erotic gateway could be getting a fun hotel on the water for the weekend or going to a sexy masquerade ball or play party.

Erotic gateways do not necessarily lead directly to sex—they may actually *be* the sexy-time activity that adds everyday eroticism to your connection with each other. Bringing in more opportunities to connect in a pleasurable way helps to build more consistent interest in sexy-time and general enjoyment of one another. More on that later.

By engaging in no-pressure, no-expectation erotic gateways together, enjoying a connective activity becomes the goal, allowing your bodies to feel safe enough to be yourself as you are and to generate those feel-good endorphins in each other's presence—safe enough and internally motivated by interest and excitement. Appreciate each other, reflecting how your partner is inspiring, attractive, fun, interesting, or just willing to try. This creates more opportunities to find attunement and flow between you, to engage in that delightful surge of aliveness alongside each other.

Erotic gateways also create more of that structure to your relationship that you had prior to a deeper commitment. Remember when you were just getting to know each other as different people with separate lives scheduling activities and intentional time together between working your job, cleaning your own house, and managing your own finances? Remember how you made space in your schedule, showered and shaved, did the sacred adornment process in anticipation of seeing each other? Those were erotic gateways, the architecture that allowed space to long for each other and cue your body to transition from the mundane to the magical. Once you moved in together and combined your lives, much of this architecture was probably lost. You stopped prioritizing the space for erotic gateways and therefore lost some of your individuality that made you interesting to each other. Weaving your lives together is an exciting and meaningful transition into love and secure attachment, but when you don't continue to make space for the shift between different settings and nervous system states, you begin to lose some of that verve and delight that transitioning into connection offers.

Prioritizing erotic gateways can be challenging for both intrinsic and extrinsic reasons. Do you feel like you often put yourself on the back burner? Or focus more on the planning and less on the experiencing? Or prioritize your partner's pleasure over yours? These are some of the intrinsic reasons you may be feeling embarrassment or lack of motivation to devote yourself to what relaxes and feels good to you. Extrinsic reasons for not investing in erotic gateways may be your stress level, hectic schedule, difficulty with childcare, a health issue that is dominating your focus, or just general overwhelm or over-commitment with the events of life. You may feel that you only have time and energy for an erotic gateway that you do on your own. Keep doing your individual erotic gateways and start to devote some time together, either trying on each other's gateways or identifying a mutual gateway that you may already be doing, but without the focus of connection. Even a trip to the grocery store can become an erotic gateway.

It's not *what* you do, it's *how* you do it.

The truth is that you can prioritize the erotic gateways that you enjoy *and* invest in the "we" of the two of you. Practice equal validation (my feelings/interests are just as important as my partner's feelings/interests, and their feelings/interests are just as important as mine). Invest in some curiosity during your mutual erotic gateway time as you allow yourself to be genuinely interested in your partner's experience. Breathe out any expectations about showing up a specific way (skillful, energetic)—allow yourself to engage slowly and invite humor if you feel awkward. If that extrinsic overwhelm just swallows up your time, invest in the small pebble erotic gateways.

Journal with your partner as you consider the following questions:

1. How do you currently transition into sexy-time?
2. What do you do with yourself to relax your body to be receptive to pleasure and connection?
3. What do you do together to relax into connection?
4. What feels both relaxing and pleasurable (first non-sexual) that you could add into your practice as a transition into sexy-time?

5. What feels accessible on work days? What feels accessible on non-work days?
6. How much time do you actually need to practice an erotic gateway? This may change based on your context and nervous system state.

Stage 2: Desire

Take a moment to visualize what desire looks and feels like to you. *Desire.* Visualize yourself standing in front of your partner and focus on something about them that you feel desire for. Notice your internal sensations—the textures, the temperature, and the movement quality. Do you notice an inner lean or inner pull toward what you desire? Does this feel physical? Emotional? Cognitive? All of the above?

Desire is the movement of arousal energy (emotional and/or sexual—both happen in the body) toward a particular direction, drawing the body and mind closer to what feels good. It can be soft, or it can be powerful and consuming. Often, desire is conflated with its adjacent feeling, lust. Physical passion and lust get the most airtime as a form of desire. In fact, you may only identify that desire is present when it is in its more powerful, consuming forms, and you may believe that this is what is expected from you or your partner to make it genuine, to make it *real desire.*

However, I find that desire can present in many forms and, unfortunately, the more subtle forms get missed or minimized, even when the feeling is genuine.

Desire can range from emotional to physical (both experienced in the felt-sense of the body and identified in the mind) and from spontaneous to responsive, and these categories can overlap. Read the descriptions and identify your typical starting point on the grid. This will help you learn what you need to bridge into the center for whole-body intimacy:

- *Emotional desire*: Feeling an inner leaning or pull toward emotional closeness and curiosity. A desire to feel emotional attunement, emotionally seen and validated, shared enjoyment and depth. Emotion is felt in the body and identified in the mind.
- *Physical desire*: Feeling an inner leaning or pull to be physically close, for skin-to-skin contact, for sexual contact. Physical desire is felt in the body and identified in the mind.
- *Spontaneous desire*: Quickly becoming interested in an emotional or sexual connection. Arousal anatomy responds more quickly to sexual stimuli.
- *Responsive desire:* It takes time and easing into connection to feel interest in emotional or sexual engagement. People in a responsive desire state want to be interested in connection but still feel stressed or mentally distracted and need to engage in an erotic gateway to relax and find the spaciousness for interest.

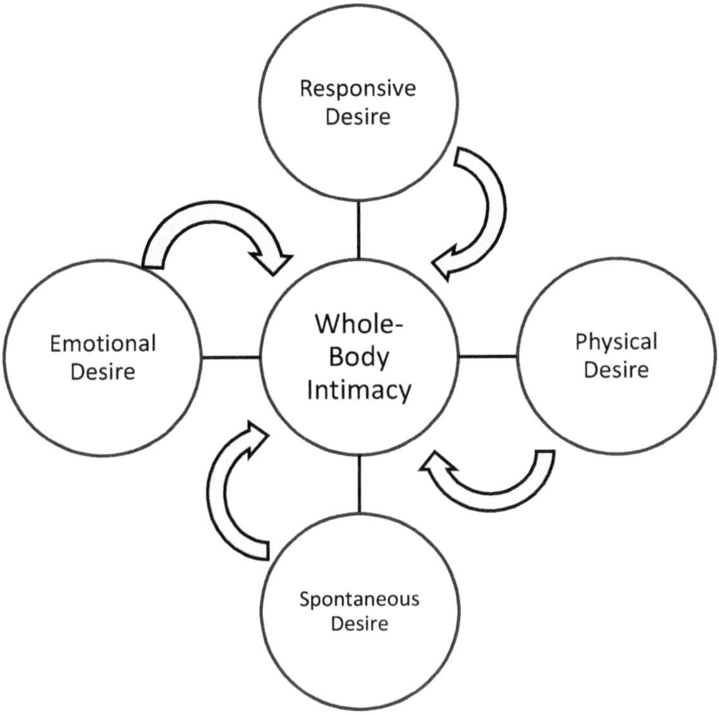

Figure 5.2 Desire Grid—Bridging Into Full-Body Intimacy.

Your location on the range of desire styles and qualities can be different from your partner because you are in different bodies with different histories and experiencing different nervous system states. Misunderstanding and miscommunication around desire can create hurt feelings and incorrect beliefs about your relational dynamic. While you may find a more consistent pattern if you were to gather data from many moments over time using this grid, the reality is that you can move about on this grid depending on your context and the state of your somatic self, and with practice, you can bridge into the center area of whole-body desire.

Desire can also show up in a non-concordant way (Nagoski, 2015)—one part of you wants to feel desire, but you are also feeling a "no" and feeling either neutral or internally retracted from connection.

This can be heartbreaking considering how many people want to feel desired by their partner or want to feel desire themselves. A desire to feel desired is a common sentiment that I hear from the couples that I work with—they say that the thing that sets an intimate relationship apart from friendships or roommates is not just sexual access but, more specifically, *feeling desired by their partner*. When this component is missing, they often find themselves questioning the validity of their partnership.

Yet, when someone feels their partner doesn't desire them, and I ask deeper questions about their experience to explore whether this is true, I often find a more subtle truth—that the person *does* feel an inner pull toward their partner, that they *do* experience desire. However, the desire presents as emotional, or they have a more responsive style, or the desire is felt within and not expressed externally due to early social conditioning that expressing passion or lust is inappropriate.

You can work as a team to unravel old conditioning that is stifling expression and support each other to cultivate embodied desire. In a committed partnership, embodied desire benefits from the body feeling both *interested* and also *safe enough* to expand, move toward, and express.

To feel *interested*, you must feel emotionally and physically differentiated enough to spark curiosity. In attachment style terms, to be differentiated is to be individuated—to feel a sense of one's own autonomy and individual personality within a relationship. In a secure attachment, you and a partner both have the space to be yourselves while also investing in shared time and values. If your relationship is in the throes of emotional entanglement or enmeshment, your blurred emotional boundaries with each other can act as a wet blanket on your capacity for desire. While it is a natural experience of your relational nervous systems to be somatically and relationally impacted by each other's feelings and actions, *entanglement* occurs when you have a hard time discerning your emotions from your partner's emotions, when you take your partner's emotions personally when they are not directed at you, or when you find yourself trying to problem-solve for your partner, so they can move past an uncomfortable emotion. Embodied desire in committed relationships has more space to move when you compassionately see yourself and your partner as individuals on your own journey, as you each experience moments of confidence and excellence, as well as moments of humanness and messiness. Encourage each other to invest in the aliveness of yourselves (your autonomy) and the aliveness of your relationship (your shared time and purpose). When this is genuine, and not out of obligation or enmeshment, you can take up space in the relationship and allow the expression of desire to flourish.

To feel *safe enough*, you benefit from knowing that you and your partner honor each other's bodily autonomy, and that you have a choice around emotional and sexual intimacy. This allows you both to feel appreciated in your sexuality so that, even if you are not in the mood for what your partner desires, you thank them for expressing it to you—while your partner may be a bit disappointed that you are not interested in intimacy, there is no pressure to engage when you don't want to. And when you do want to engage, your own embodied desire will be felt in full color. Expression of physical or emotional desire when it is genuine and consensual is a really lovely, satisfying thing. The body feels safe enough to find and express desire when you do not feel overwhelmed by the desire of the partner and obligated to rise to the occasion. So, make space for your different desire styles, be descriptive about your own, and validate the desire that your partner expresses to you and receives from you.

Let's explore your relationships to desire and how to make space for both of you for embodied experience and expression.

Experiential—Explore Your Desire Dynamic

Stand facing your partner with about 5 feet between you. Begin with your gaze soft on the floor in front of you or eyes closed, whatever feels safe enough and allows you to turn your attention inward. Take a full breath in, expanding your ribcage and belly, and on the out breath, allow any movement—stretches, twitches, and shaking out—that happens as your body settles in. Take another full breath in, expand your ribcage, belly, and back body, and a long out breath as your muscles and bones soften with gravity. On your next full breath in, expand your inner somatic landscape and turn your attention inward, noticing the sensations that awaken in your body, and on your out-breath, invite your attention to settle in. Find a baseline sensation, something that feels grounding and orienting to you. It could be the sensation of your feet on the floor, the soft sensation of your in-breath and out-breath, the sound of the birds outside, or the smell of dinner in the oven in the next room.

On your next in-breath, extend your senses to feel your partner across from you. As you feel their presence in the room, notice the sensations that begin to awaken in your body. Allow your senses to take them in and breathe them in. When you are ready, open your eyes to see them. In-breath and out-breath. Notice how you feel about this person, your beloved. What feels attractive about them in this moment? Perhaps you find them physically attractive, and perhaps you feel attracted to something about their personality or emotional quality. Notice the sensations that awaken in your body in response to focusing on something attractive about them. Can you feel that inner lean toward them? Let that inner lean move you toward them and, when you both feel ready, take turns taking a step closer to each other. Instead of making contact, allow the feeling of wanting to be closer to circulate within you. Breathe into your back body, expanding your spine, ribcage, and back of the heart, and soften your heels into the floor. Soften the muscles in your face. Share with your partner how it feels to have them take a step toward you and circulate their desire within. If your partner's pace feels faster than yours, ask them to slow down and take a step back. It is normal to have different paces—explore how to move at the pace of genuine connection. Once you have stepped back and are able to feel yourself and your desire to move toward again, let yourself be moved by the inner impulse. If your partner needs to take a step back to connect with themselves again, tell them that you trust their bodily autonomy (remember embodied consent and the body autonomy practice?). Then switch, allowing the other to take a step forward, letting the movement originate from the sensation of emotional or physical desire in your body. Share with your partner the impact of having them step closer and soften around their desire.

Thank each other for sharing, and then journal and talk about the following questions:

- Where within your body is your desire coming from? What is it that your desire is moving toward?
- What did your desire hope would happen?
- How did the sensation of desire change when you stepped closer without touching?
- What was the somatic impact of your partner stepping closer to you from their own desire?
- What sensations did you feel when they stepped back before switching to your turn?
- Were you able to keep track of your own body as you engaged in the experience? If this felt challenging, what was helpful to bring you back to your body? Returning to focus on your breath? Focusing on something outside yourself for a moment, like your favorite plant? Remember that consciousness is expensive, so support your body awareness to ebb in and out and back again.

This experiential incorporates the practice of embodied consent. Notice the impact of containment and circulation of desire and its importance in giving your partner space to receive your desire and respond.

Stage 3: Arousal

Often accompanying and amplifying desire, arousal is your experience of the pleasurable sensations that your peripheral and central arousal anatomy are wired for. You are full of sensitive nerve-filled tissues, ready to respond to your preferred kind of touch. It has a series of stages, from unaroused to low arousal, culminating in a heightened altered state of pleasure, a sense of timelessness, and lowered inhibitions, with the final stage a transition out of arousal into a resting state. The stages of arousal are the undercurrent that runs throughout the whole sexual response experience.

These nerve-filled tissues throughout your arousal anatomy are also wired to detect discomfort and danger and will redirect energy away from pleasure into protection at a moment's notice, faster than the speed at which your cognitive mind can pick up on what is happening.

Arousal can build, it can soften, it can get interrupted, and it can build again. This brilliant force in the body is creative energy. It is inspiring and powerful, and your relationship benefits from you learning how to use it wisely.

Arousal anatomy is sensitive and wise, and you can learn to be awake in the altered state of arousal to amplify it, contain it, and release it. When we are not awake in our arousal, we can be swept up in free flow and miss the cues from a partner that they want to slow down or that they have become uncomfortable, so learning to be awake and aware in arousal, combined with the practice of embodied consent, can help lower the potential of such disconnection and misunderstanding. We can also be disconnected from the feeling of arousal with too much bound flow in the muscles and tissues of the somatic nervous system, blocking our access to it, or causing us to grip too tightly to the need for release, or orgasming before we are ready, as it slips from our ability to modulate.

In order to facilitate the building and modulating of arousal energy, sometimes you only need to relax and breathe into the sensitive areas of your body. Other times, vigorous erotic gateways are needed to clear the body of stress—which can happen in the case of arousal non-concordance—in order to make way for arousal energy. Sex educator Emily Nagoski (2015) refers to this as a state of feeling both a break and an accelerator at the same time—one part of you feels arousal, interest, or desire for sexual intimacy (accelerator) and other parts of you feel either internally neutral or retracted (brake). Arousal non-concordance is a normal and necessary mechanism in the body, refining your arousal anatomy's ability to discern what sexual situations are the most reasonable, the most interesting, and the most genuinely pleasurable. If part of you has the brake on, it's time to look around for the obstacle and discover what it needs to be able to hit the accelerator again. Just as in driving a car, hitting the accelerator while still pressing the brake won't get you very far. We will discuss this more in the next chapter on sexuality challenges.

If you or your partner has trauma organization in your body built from traumatic prior experiences, you may notice that your arousal anatomy can abruptly turn off sensation, cause pain or muscle tension in arousal anatomy, and prevent orgasm or cause orgasm to happen before you are ready, heightening discomfort and preventing the following stages of sexual responsiveness. This is like your body pulling the emergency brake suddenly during sex—something has triggered a sense of danger within you, and your body has taken immediate steps to protect. Practice embodied consent here—slow down, speak simply, and give time for you or your partner's nervous system to regulate. Over time, the body can heal some of this trauma organization when the connection with a partner consistently feels safe enough, and you engage regulation and resilience skills to return to your window of capacity. It is crucial that you feel you have a choice to start, stop, or slow down, and that you feel validated in your feelings or discomfort. When you receive this kind of compassionate holding experience, the body will often soften and begin to lean in again. Take your time here. Slow down to make progress. Resource early, resource often.

Experiential—Embodied Exploration of Arousal Response

Breathe into peripheral arousal anatomy, then into central arousal anatomy. Expand these sensitive areas of your body with breath, yielding and softening the body on the out-breath, feeling the impact of gravity over time. As you breathe in and breathe out, notice how your tissues expand and soften. Notice the transition space between peripheral and central arousal anatomy within your somatic landscape. With your inner awareness, locate the different body structures and how they are all intricately linked through skin and muscle tissues, connected through vascular networks and sensory pathways of nerves. Follow with your awareness of sensation the pathway from the tips of your toes, inch by inch, up through your whole body, all the way to the crown of your head. Notice how the structure of your body, the architecture of bones, holds and makes space for all the beautiful tissues and organs that allow you to feel. You may notice warmth building in your body, you may notice arousal, and you may also notice discomfort. In-breath and out-breath. Breathe appreciation into your whole body for its capacity to feel, to expand, and to receive.

Try this in different contexts. Begin with a solo exploration, then maybe add some ambient music or audio erotica (not visual erotica, as it takes you out of deep connection with your somatic landscape into a highly visual ocular-lock). Once you feel ready, you can explore with your partner. Invite your partner to place their hand on areas of your peripheral and then central arousal anatomy. Practice embodied consent. Only use stillness touch during this experiential (see chapter on Bodyful Touch), as this practice is not about stimulation but about awareness and appreciation.

Stage 4: Flow Space

The flow space during your sexy-time is the moment or moments where your nervous systems have balanced together, fluidly alternating the tension and release of muscles, each following movement impulse while attuning to each other.

Like water flowing around rock, pleasurable physiological arousal has given rise to the free-flow of movement, softening any awkwardness or hesitance. Flow space is like two quad skaters on the rink, holding hands. One passes the other and then pulls the other forward, meeting together again. It's exhilarating and relaxing at the same time.

It is the structure of the shared movement dynamic itself, your genuine improvisational choreography, that is holding you within a flow pattern as you actively yield into the rhythm, moving and being moved at the same time.

Flow space is not possible without a transition space giving time for the nervous system to build arousal and momentum, the gathering of moments of tension and compelling excitement that are followed by a release of endorphins and feel-good neurochemicals. Pain recedes to the background as arousal builds together, causing aching bodies to soften, awkwardness and inhibition to smooth over, and a sense of timelessness takes over. Flow space is the body entering into a kind of rhythmic trance, an altered state that softens the muscular and nervous system inhibitions of the body and increases the proximity to peak moments and orgasm. This is the release moment in true *eroticism.* After you have followed your interest and excitement through any obstacles or challenges, and you arrive at the flow space—compelled to move through tension to release—you are lifted up with pleasurable buoyancy.

The immersive experience of the flow space of sexuality is akin to the psychological theory of *flow* as articulated by Mihály Csikszentmihalyi (2009). Csíkszentmihályi did something very important to our understanding of happiness—he emphasized that happiness is not something that just happens or is dependent on luck. Instead, happiness is cultivated through our diligent dedication to activities that we genuinely enjoy, training and participating in the things that both take effort and have intrinsic value to us. By immersing ourselves in such experiences, we can access the nervous system state of flow where distractions fall away, and the activity compels our attention with a full-body pleasurable focus. This is not a passive experience but an embodied and active participation in what gives us a sense of aliveness.

Flow space can begin during erotic gateways and can carry over into your experience and expression of desire, all the way through peak moments and integration. Follow whatever compels your focus with embodied pleasure and your dance of movement impulses with consent—without consent, the inner discomfort of a "no" as in arousal non-concordance would prevent the body from releasing into a flow state. Accessing flow space is easier for some than others, so practice compassion with yourself and with your partner if this feels difficult. Flow space can be a moment in time or a series of moments that gather momentum and culminate in a period of attunement between people. Also referred to as *rhythmic entrainment,* flow space and orgasm rely on rhythmic oscillations within your nervous system, between you and your partner's nervous systems, and between your parasympathetic (rest and digest) and sympathetic (activation and action) branches of the nervous system. In this state, your brain is releasing both oxytocin (the relaxation and bonding hormone) and vasopressin (a vasodilator that increases heart rate and keeps you alert). When you and your partner are both motivated by pleasure and practicing consent, researchers believe that sexual rhythms are likely to entrain synchronous brain oscillations (Safron, 2016), making the somatic attunement feel like a mutual experience—moving as one. This is what people refer to when they describe a sense of transcendent union or *oneness.*

Here is something for you to try that can help you access an experience of flow space.

Experiential—Flow Space

Sit or stand facing your partner and place your pointer fingers from your dominant hand together. Full breath in, long breath out. Begin with a balance between your fingers, gently resting the pad of your finger to your partner's. Feel the give of your partner's finger. Notice how it feels within your somatic landscape to connect in this new way and then extend your senses to feel your partner in space with you. Slow your awareness to feel your own pulse and the pulse from your partner's finger. Notice the relationship between your pulses—you are beginning to attune.

When you are ready and/or your pulses align, one of you will slowly begin guiding the other by pressing your finger into theirs, pulling back, flowing to the side, and so on. If you are standing, you can guide your partner to change levels, flow around each other, and return to stillness for a moment before moving again. Keep your pointer fingers connected throughout and, if you lose connection, take a breath and invite each other back to connect fingers again. Once one partner feels complete in their guiding (maybe five minutes or so), switch to the other partner guiding the movement. Remember not to push your partner too fast or too hard or try to trick them by changing directions too quickly—this is about inviting and practicing feeling each other while following one person's movement impulse.

Once you both have had a designated turn guiding, return to stillness together and then trade off who is leading/guiding. What is the pace that is needed to stay in contact as you follow one person's movement impulse to completion, as the other person's movement impulse guides the next movement to completion? In-breath and out-breath, back and forth, follow one partner's movement impulse and let it flow into the next person's movement impulse until there is no beginning or ending to the flowing exchange between you.

Once you have tried this with your fingertips, you can try this exercise with your whole hand, forearm, side bodies, and so on, in the style of contact improv dance. Remember to move at the pace of connection, to practice embodied consent, and return to stillness from time to time to check in with yourselves and each other (adapted from Jackson, 2022).

Take a few moments to explore these journal prompts together after this experiential:

1. What do you appreciate about the connection you just experienced?
2. What sensations and emotions did you feel as you lead? As you followed?
3. What helped you stay connected?
4. At what point did you feel disconnected? And how did you find your way back into connection?
5. If you noticed you had different paces (speeds), at what point did you notice that you started moving at the pace of connection?
6. At what point did you feel moments of flow—a sense of immersion and timelessness?

Stage 5: Peak Moments

Ecstasy. Transcendence. Euphoria. *Orgasm.* Often identified as the *goal* of sex, orgasm is elevated as the pinnacle of sexual connection. However, many sex therapists and sex educators encourage people to de-center orgasm as the goal to reach in favor of more attainable, realistic, and personally meaningful benchmarks. "Achieving" orgasm is an unrealistic goal for some people, and for others, centering orgasm makes orgasm itself more difficult by putting pressure on people to feel a sense of failure, embarrassment, or shame if they or a partner does not have an orgasm during sex. This kind of pressure is dysregulating to the nervous system, dropping the body into a fight/flight/freeze/fawn response that inhibits relaxation and redirects the blood and oxygen necessary for arousal away from arousal anatomy.

There are a few truths about genital orgasms during partner sex for you and a partner to know:

- Orgasms are a team effort.
- Orgasms are not and should not be an expectation or benchmark for good sex.
- Access to orgasms changes over your lifespan due to emotional, physical, medical, relationship, and hormonal factors.
- Orgasm can be a protective response to protect the body or release intense stress.
- Orgasm most often happens once rhythmic stimulation has reached flow space with heightened arousal levels.
- Orgasm can also happen spontaneously while sleeping, while exercising, while meditating, while fantasizing, and so on, without any physical stimulation at all.
- Oscillate your awareness between you and your partner. Orgasms don't happen, or don't happen when you want to, if you are only focused on

your partner rather than on your own pleasure. Everyone has to be motivated by physical and emotional pleasure.
- Orgasms are not the only form of peak moments!

Peak moments are identified as any moment or moments when you feel that ecstatic spark of pleasure with your partner. This could be an emotional rapture, a physical climax of pleasure, an ecstatic taste while sharing beautiful food, or a transcendent vision in your mind during intimacy. When you and an intimate partner shift the goal of sex from orgasm to an intention for attunement, these kinds of peak moments become possible. The rhythmic entrainment of your nervous systems in the flow space builds when introducing an exciting element, such as fantasy or extra physical stimulation, until arousal amplifies to an ecstatic culmination. Once that climactic threshold is met, relaxing the body into the continuing rhythm sends waves of pleasure through the whole somatic landscape.

The ability to rhythmically entrain nervous systems in excited states with a partner is more likely when you cultivate spaces to experience this kind of attunement *outside* of the sexually intimate space. Rhythmic entrainment can happen during a tennis match, while dancing together, playing a tabletop game, singing, hiking, or cuddling together, among many other activities—anything that allows you to feel the flow space rhythm between you, and which amplifies your enjoyment of each other's company. These peak moments validate your relationship and remind you of your life-affirming connection with each other.

Journal with your partner about the following:

1. Name at least three different ways that you have experienced peak moments together.
2. What are the descriptive qualities of these peak moments? Identify sensations, movement qualities, qualities of attention, and breath qualities.
3. Name your "gasm!" Examples are "hiking-gasm," "vision-gasm," or "food-gasm."

Stage 6: Integration

The moments after sexy-time provide an opportunity to reflect on the experience and emotionally lift each other up at a time when your bodies are wide open and sensitized. After the sensory landscape of the body is amplified through arousal, expression of desire, and the rhythmic entrainment or dissonance of nervous systems, the body and heart are open to deeper emotions. This is the phase of exploring what helps transition out of the altered state of arousal in a way that is re-regulating to the nervous system and co-regulating between intimate partners.

Sometimes, this sensitized time is when you feel most connected to your partner as you relax into the echoes of pleasurable sensations from waves of endorphins, dopamine, and oxytocin that flooded your body. You may feel the freedom of being unmasked—seeing your partner and being seen in your most raw and primal form. You also might feel relief from pain as you relax your muscles and bones, or you might feel a relief from feeling disconnected from your partner, knowing you will now enjoy a period of time feeling more attuned to each other.

Other times, this is a vulnerable time of feeling the complex emotions that are inherent in a socialized sexuality. You may find that you feel unsure about how your partner feels about the experience you just shared, or you might feel disappointed in your experience. You may feel some embarrassment or shame about what was expressed as a desire or a request that you made. You may be feeling disappointed or hurt when, for example, arousal non-concordance surfaced and presented a challenge, your partner didn't notice or respond to your need to slow down because they were in a highly aroused state.

While it is normal and common that challenges and difficult feelings arise during intimate partner sexy-time, the dominant culture stereotype that sex should be natural causes us to feel all kinds of insecurities and can induce dysregulation in the nervous system. You may find yourself feeling critical of yourself or your partner, or feeling confusion or fear, and thus feeling more disconnected than before you started.

If you have experienced prior trauma or violation, the transition out of arousal can activate the trauma organization of the body, replacing the pleasurable sensations with difficult emotions that cause your body to retract or become flooded.

An intentional practice of integration following sexy-time provides a space for you and your intimate partner to optimize this period of body-heart sensitivity to nourish your connection with each other, to bolster your self-perceptions, and to do some deep learning and maturing. This is a time of *after-care*—a time to take care of your emotions and nervous systems so that, even if challenges arise during sexy-time, you can feel seen with love, respected, and connected as you tend to each other's well-being.

Integration is a time to share appreciation and celebrate what was surprising and fun. Perhaps you learned something new about your body, your connection, or you had a vision during your peak moment.

It is also a time to process a moment when you felt dysregulated or disconnected or to share a kind of touch or pace that didn't feel good. When your partner shares something that was challenging, make sure to appreciate them for telling you something so vulnerable. Revisit the embodied communication principles we explored earlier. People often don't want to hurt their partner's feelings and don't want their partner to take anything personally. Remember that when a partner shares something that didn't feel good or activated dysregulation, they are not criticizing you or your desires. Just because it didn't feel good doesn't mean that you did anything wrong. It was just not the right time to speed the pace up or to switch activities because your nervous systems were in different states or stages. It could also mean that your partner had an old and painful body memory emerge, such as an old wound from a prior relationship or a wound from a challenging time earlier in your relationship. The sensitizing of the body through arousal and skin-to-skin contact can sometimes activate the painful experiences of prior abuse or relational hurts, not to re-injure us but to allow us an opportunity to heal. Wounding happens in a relationship; therefore, healing must happen in the relationship too. Rupture and repair. And when the wound feels deep, as in prior infidelity or not having been present for your partner emotionally after a traumatic or difficult experience, the healing requires a *rupture* to be followed by *repair, repair, repair*. This isn't about saying sorry forever, but it is about telling your partner, *that makes sense* that a painful feeling or memory came up and *thank you for telling me*. Embracing your partner's sharing of a challenge allows them to feel safe enough to soften the body armor, be transparent and genuine, and process difficult feelings while in connection. Repair within the integration stage after sexy-time will help to heal these old wounds and—bonus!—improve your sexy-time in the future.

It is also important to honor each other's styles of connection at this time for the after-care to be truly received. Some of you may be more *independence first* types (Atkinson, 2005), where your nervous system needs a bit of time with low stimulation after sexy-time before connecting with your partner again. You may benefit from going to the bathroom, getting a drink of water, stretching, or showering so that your nervous system can settle again, allowing you to come back to connected integration with a partner. Others of you may be *togetherness first* types and feel emotional and nervous system regulation from staying physically connected to a partner after sexy-time. Having different styles here is normal and is less about how you feel about each other or the experience and more about how your nervous system is organized after a highly stimulating sexual encounter.

Take a moment to explore with each other and come up with a few things to try together to make the after-care of sexy-time a more integrating experience.

Ask yourself and your partner:

- Do you prefer to be close after sexy-time, or do you need a few moments to yourself?
- If you prefer to be close, do you enjoy some quiet time first, or do you like to dive into talking about what you enjoyed, what you were surprised by,

or processing a moment where you felt dysregulated or disconnected to share appreciations and validations?

- If you prefer to have a few moments to yourself, does your nervous system benefit from an activity such as a shower, a bite to eat, or a drink? Or do you benefit from rest like taking a nap?

Once you share your answers, thank each other for sharing, and explore how you can work together as a team to allow both of you to have nervous systems that are receptive to the after-care. Perhaps when the person who needs a bit of solo time takes a shower, the partner who desires connection can take this time to place their hands on their own body to breathe in self-love and self-validation or journal about their experience. This is a great opportunity to practice secure attachment with themselves. Make sure that you have a few moments to come back together and, if you don't have much time (you might be late for work!), just share one appreciation with each other. Then do a full integration later that night or the next day. With your busy schedules, it is important to practice compassion and incorporate this practice in a way that feels doable so that you can prioritize this important stage.

Somatosensory Experience at the Center

Your somatic experience and relational expression at each stage can be amplified or inhibited (or both at the same time) based on your prior learning that teaches you whether and how you can experience and express your sexuality. We all receive both clear and surreptitious messages about sex and intimacy through immersion in the social environments of family, culture, religion, peer group, and popular culture. Some of these messages are supportive of a healthy, life-giving relationship with the body and sexuality and can be a source of strength and connection. Unfortunately, many of the messages and experiences subvert bodily autonomy and inhibit healthy, enjoyable sexual connection.

For example, if you have grown up in conservative purity culture, you probably got the message that exploring sexuality prior to marriage is forbidden, so, once you are married, you probably also learned that sexual intelligence doesn't magically materialize (Sutter, 2024). You have discovered, or will discover, that you have a lot of learning to do to unravel the restrictive patterns that your body has formed in response to the teachings. You will also have to unlearn your assumptions about sexual behavior and desires based on gender and your role in an intimate relationship. While religion is a positive force and a community refuge for many people, it may also promote confusing and shaming perspectives about sexuality that creates both interpersonal turmoil and intra-personal conflict.

The somatic burden of this messaging often manifests as discomfort during intimacy, sexual avoidance, sexual pain, deep embarrassment, and even infidelity, eating disorders, anxiety, and out-of-control sexual behavior.

Erotically marginalized people, such as LGBTQ and racial minority couples, often experience relationship stress from the impact of the overt and covert messages from the dominant culture (Bos et.al., 2021; Cao et.al., 2017). The impact of this can lead to avoidance of emotional intimacy in sexual relationships, as well as sexual challenges such as pain during sex, hyper- or hypo-tone in the muscles of the body, or secret-keeping and infidelity, due to the validity of sexual identity being minimized and marginalized.

By exploring the whole-person sexual response cycle together, you can begin to identify where your early teachings have benefited you and where they have injured you and therefore inhibited your sexual expression. You can work as a team to support each other to unravel challenges and misunderstandings, identify your resilience, and co-create a safe enough space to enjoy a personally meaningful sexual intimacy. Together, you can invest in erotic gateways, incorporate embodied consent, allow the body to volumize with arousal and desire, become immersed in flow space, heighten excitement and release into peak moments, and share the vulnerability of your personal experience during integration. And when a challenge surfaces, you can, with compassion, make space to unravel the painful learning that has kept you at arm's length from your sexual connection. Sex itself shouldn't be painful—it should be pleasurable, consensual, and meaningful.

To explore your challenges, pay attention to your somatosensory experience at each stage of sexual response—from erotic gateways to integration. When you are able to identify in your body where you are getting stuck, you now have something tangible to work with. Perhaps you don't have an alternative to a negative belief or body memory that you carry, but, in a safe-enough environment, you can directly work with uncomfortable sensations to offer relief, find some integration, and create new somatic pathways for greater comfort and pleasure. This allows a new experience and new belief to unfold and create a more life-affirming perspective on your sexual response.

Here are a few sensations that can be effective starting points. Notice, when do you feel:

- Uncomfortable tension in your muscles or abdomen
- Tension around your heart, such as a sudden increase or decrease in speed
- Losing attunement with your partner
- An increase in body pain
- Your mind losing focus, feeling "floaty" or intensely distracted
- Feeling overwhelmed, overstimulated, or "flooded" with confusing sensations

- Your quality of attention becoming rigidly narrow and fixated on something uncomfortable
- An intense need to stop or leave the room
- Tight, wiggly sensations in your abdomen

These are all indications that your body is experiencing a "no"—a body memory is surfacing and needs you to slow down and tend to it by validating why you may be feeling this sensation, perhaps by completing an action, movement, or verbal communication that feels stuck, and then offering an alternative perspective on the health of your expression.

Let's explore two examples.

Daniela and Cory

After Daniela and Cory, both in their late 40s, had a great time at pickleball (erotic gateway) with friends, they went home to shower (erotic gateway), and have some private time together (intentional sexy-time) before a planned dinner with Daniela's work colleagues. While both decided on no expectations for genital contact, as Daniela became more aroused throughout the shower, Cory started to feel a tightening around his chest. They transitioned to the bed together, and Daniela initiated some caressing touch along Cory's body, and he noticed his body was becoming more hyper-tonic (increased muscle tension). Daniela noticed too and said to Cory, "let's slow down and breathe." Cory lets her know that he is feeling tension in his chest and does need a few moments to breathe and see what the "no" is about. "I was really looking forward to this time with you, so I don't know what this is about!" Daniela brought her hands to stillness on Cory's chest as she took a few deep breaths in and out, slowing her pace and circulating her arousal within her body. Cory breathed into his chest, expanding to press into Daniela's hands, asking the tension in his chest what it is trying to do for him. He realized that the tension was trying to protect him by retracting from an uncomfortable situation—he realized that he was concerned about whether he would be able to maintain an erection.

Cory had recently visited his doctor because he had been feeling fatigue, lack of focus, and his erections were happening less frequently. His doctor talked to him about his age and decided to test his testosterone, but no treatments or solutions had been offered yet. The tension in his chest was protecting him from engaging in a situation where he would have to feel his uncertainty and be witnessed in however his body responds. He had recently been flooded with critical thoughts that he had heard over his life about masculinity as men age. This felt really vulnerable to Cory, as shaky anxiousness filled his belly and his muscles tightened around his heart like a shield. Cory then took another breath in and asked his chest what it needed to soften and open to his partner. "I don't know if I can do what I've been taught I should be able to do," his tight muscles told him, "I don't know if I'm enough." He realized he needed to restate with Daniela the "no expectations" and that this is about pleasure and connection, so he can learn what his body needs. He shared this with Daniela, and she thanked him for sharing with her, restating that this time is about pleasure and connection, not expectations, and she suggested they share some no-pressure erotic massage (a desire for both).

They had previously developed the "no expectations" agreement when Daniela was doing personal work on deconstructing her Catholic upbringing related to sex. While she still loved her faith, she recognized that the messages related to sexuality were damaging. She had been experiencing pain in her pelvic floor connected with a strong sense of shame, and the "no expectations" allowed her the space to tend to her body, validate her desires for her partner, and eventually softened the pain while increasing their intimacy and trust in each other. So, as Daniela slowed down with Cory, he was able to take a long breath out and, as they relaxed together with some sensual touch and his erection ebbed and flowed, both focused on pleasure until they found themselves in the flow space. Cory then found that his arousal built to an erection that allowed them to have some enjoyable penetrative sex.

Whether or not physiological changes are medical, centering pleasure and connection over body performance goals allows the nervous system to find the balance of relaxation and excitement. This allows you to access a good sexual connection even in the presence of uncertainty. Over time, it also allows you to unravel inaccurate and unhelpful sexuality narratives so you can break out of the assumptions that prevent you from really connecting with your partner. You get to define your sexuality for yourself, based on what is true, meaningful, and consensual.

Serena and Jenn

Serena (52) and Jenn (45) have been married for about 8 years, and 2 years ago, Jenn had a sexual connection with a former partner that was outside of her relationship agreements with Serena. As non-monogamous partners, they had agreed to date other people and to have a conversation before they are sexual with anyone else. Along with other agreements, this transparency had allowed their secure attachment dynamic to flourish as they navigated honest and congruent communication, practiced validating each other's bodily autonomy and feelings, and prioritized balancing intentional time together with solo time. So, when Jenn connected sexually with her prior partner and Serena discovered this through a mutual friend, the trust they had developed ruptured. Jenn had been hesitant to tell her she had reconnected with an old flame who had been unkind to Jenn in the past and didn't want to follow Serena and Jenn's relationship agreements.

As they continue to work toward healing this relational wound, a memory of this broken agreement has started to surface for Serena during their flow space. Serena noticed that she feels a painful retraction in her solar plexus and a sudden tunnel vision in her attention that shocks her out of the flow when they are connecting intimately. Serena shares in their couples session: "We're in the flow, and then a sudden shift happens where I feel like I don't know Jenn, like she's a stranger, and my body just shuts down." As Serena breathes around the echo of this sensation in her body, I invite her to notice what this sensation is trying to tell her—what is this inner "no" about? I notice Serena curl into the midline of her body, her hands over her chest and upper abdomen. Her voice is tight, both angry and sad, as she says, "I thought I could trust her, but I don't know who that is now." Jenn turns to me and says, "I don't know how many times I have to say sorry about this. I've told her what happened and she can't let it go." Visibly frustrated, Jenn appeared exasperated, eyes wide, head shaking, her hands a wall between her and her partner. I encouraged Jenn to slow down. This is a moment to lean in to support both of them to practice finding congruence in the moment—they have reaffirmed their agreements and done good work to support their emotional bodies and communicate openly again, but the somatic body still has layers to unravel and integrate. The trauma of the rupture takes longer to heal because this is the innate survival mechanism that is working to keep Serena safe. Consistency in presence helps to ease this automatic nervous system armoring in the moment. I encourage Jenn to turn toward Serena and let her know what makes sense about why she's feeling this retraction and body memory at the flow state moments in their intimacy. After taking a few full breaths in and long breaths out, Jenn turns to Serena, seeing her retracted posture and deep sadness, and tells her, "It makes sense that you feels this shock when we are in the flow because you've told me previously that that is when you feel the most vulnerable which was a raw, euphoric experience before the rupture. I wonder if that vulnerability opens you up to more hurt. Did I get that right?" Serena tightened even more for a moment and then let out a long breath and said, "Yes, you are the first person that I've been able to open up to like that, to really let go and just float. But I still have moments where it's not safe to be vulnerable with you." I asked Serena where else this feels familiar from. Serena paused for a few moments and recalled memories of her younger-hood when her mom continued to find out about the affairs of her father, which initiated a cycle of fighting and separations between her parents, creating a lot of instability for her and her family. Jenn softened and leaned closer to Serena as she shared and then said, "I am right here with you and I really value creating stability with you." Serena's face and shoulders softened as she reached for Jenn's hand: "Thank you for saying that." I encouraged them to follow the next movement impulse as they connected both of their hands, pulling each other in for a hug. I encouraged breathing together, finding each other's pulse, and softening into the moment. In this reconnection, they returned to their erotic gateway of breathing with each other.

After any kind of rupture, once apologies have been exchanged, the circumstances explained, and new agreements are made, the deeper somatic healing still needs to be done. This cannot be done through talking about it. It must be tended to in the moments that it arises. Slowing down in these moments to validate the feelings, regulate your nervous systems so that you can widen and soften any rigid thinking (criticism, judgment, and shame), and restating agreements and values allows the healing to settle into a more open and receptive somatic landscape. Over time, these moments will gather stability in the body memory bank to counteract the body memory of rupture and betrayal. Identifying your "yes" in your connection with each other as you discover somatosensory experiences that feel like strengths in the cycle of sexual responsiveness allows you to celebrate where your intimacy feels easeful and full-bodied. These are the places that embody what Dance Movement Therapists call *full effort expression*—expression that feels more fully coordinated and easefully confident. Notice your stages of sexual responsiveness that often go well and are sources of inspiration and positive reflection between you. This "yes" might come from the moments when you have successfully worked through a "no," as in the experience of the two couples described earlier. The "yes" might also come from the excitement of sharing a new experience with each other and investing in more personally meaningful ways of connecting sexually.

Simon and Clara

Simon (37) and Clara (42) recently started doing cold plunges together as a way to connect around a fun challenge and to benefit their health. They realized that the initial dip felt like a full-body orgasm as they gasped, willing their body to breathe deeply and relax into the cold for a few minutes. They found that they often felt euphoric as they emerged from the icy water. Before their newfound cold plunge journey, Clara had been having difficulty with her peak moment stage of sexual response, the emotional and physical heights muted recently, probably due to the onset of perimenopause. After a few weeks of plunging, they connected sexually and, as they arrived at the flow space, Clara felt the impulse to replicate the cold plunge breath. Clara's body capacity for intensity had expanded through her experiences in the cold water, and she felt her muscles and lungs, her inner somatic landscape, longing to widen. She took a deep breath in, expanding her ribcage and elongating her spine, and then fully relaxed her body. She repeated this a few times as her arousal built, widening her capacity for the peak experience. This sensation alone felt euphoric. And after a few instances of doing this body-breath practice during sexy-time, Clara had her first genital orgasm in months. During the integration phases, they appreciated each other for being interested in a new practice together that had opened her sexuality potential again.

This kind of sensory play can increase your capacity for sensing and feeling as well as your range of movement and expressiveness. Engaging in an activity that invites a new somatic experience expands your movement repertoire by deepening your capacity for movements you already know or learning new movement pathways that offer you an alternative to outdated habits that have begun to inhibit a fresh experience. Our bodies are wired to respond to new experiences through the brilliant mechanism of adaptation—our bodies love an interesting problem to solve, a fun challenge to engage with. This is why humans are attracted to games of all kinds: sports, tabletop gaming, the morning Wordle game in the New York Times, pickleball, and so on. We get a cascade of endorphins and dopamine when we engage in an activity that causes some good stress, followed by release through finding flow in the activity or post-activity relaxation. I will talk more about this in the next section.

Miles and Alex

*Miles (32) and Alex (35) found that their sexual connection had started feeling more transactional, and they wanted to experience a more engaging and meaningful connection. A couple that they were friends with recommended listening to ethical audio erotica that had interesting narratives and used more descriptive language—less explicitly sexual and more sensory-based. They started with a fantasy-based novel on an audio streaming service that they could sit on the couch together and listen to over their sound system. The story had great intro and transition music, and the narrator's voice sounded engaging. As they listened, they shared with each other that the language felt so visceral and accessible, not over-the-top. It was edgy in a sensory way—*they could feel the words as they were being read *(remember embodied communication?). During their integration phase after sexy-time, Miles and Alex started appreciating each other and sharing their experience in this more descriptive language. They found that they could feel the somatic and emotional qualities of each other more deeply. This deeper understanding allowed them to access their somatic attunement with each other more frequently, so their sexy-time rarely felt transactional anymore.*

When sexy-time is feeling less intimate and more paint-by-numbers, look just a little outside the box for inspiration. Often, finding something adjacent to your way of engaging can open up options that you didn't know were there. Miles and Alex were no strangers to erotic entertainment, but erotic fantasy that uses more embodied language was new, interesting, and ultimately inspirational.

Apply This Model to Your Everyday Eroticism

Many of my clients arrive on my couch with reasons why genital-centric sex is difficult or off the table: one partner may be in the middle of a trauma-healing process, or they may have a medical condition that makes sex painful (such as lichen sclerosis). Or, there has been a lapse in their sexual connection because they have been through the process of pregnancy, childbirth, and adjusting to life with an infant, so they are feeling too disconnected and uncertain to jump back into regular sexual connection.

Maybe sex is difficult for you right now due to life factors or health reasons. Or maybe your sexual connection is just fine, and you want to keep it thriving by adding in non-sexual, inspiring ways of connecting. The whole-person sexual response cycle can lead to entrained nervous systems in everyday situations that can be just as satisfying as sexual connection.

This six-stage model of sexual responsiveness isn't just for sex. As I mentioned in the erotic gateways chapter, everyday eroticism can be a meaningful way to connect outside of the typical definition of sex in non-overtly sexual ways that still take you through the stages of erotic gateways, desire, arousal, flow space, peak moments, and integration. This cycle is architecture for the rhythm of the creative, life force energy of your body, and it is found in many different forms and contexts in your daily life. By exploring and refining this rhythm in many facets of your life, you can clarify and amplify your somatic pathways of pleasure and life-affirming expression.

Remember Daniela and Cory playing pickleball? Or Simon and Clara doing cold plunges? Both of these activities involve *erotic gateways* (getting ready, gathering their gear, warming up, stretching, encouraging each other), *desire* (they feel a building of excitement as they anticipate how good they will feel during and/or after the activity), *arousal* (their physiological response to these two challenging and pleasurable activities), *flow space* (the moments of flow as they work together to get the ball over the net or the moments when their bodies relax in the cold water as they begin to sway and breath more easefully), *peak moments* (that first gasp of the cold plunge or the euphoria as they exit the water, or the moments of laughter and elation when they score in pickleball), and, of course, *integration* (recounting exciting or triumphant moments of the game, appreciating each other, or relaxing in the hot tub after either activity).

Participating in activities like these pleasure practices allows you both to feel the cycle of the pleasurable building and releasing of energy together. You both feel good in your bodies at the same time as you share in active engagement. This is nervous system entrainment, with the exciting peaks and releases that are also accessible in the space of sexual intimacy, and it can generate a meaningful and life-affirming experience.

Talk with your partner about starting a new challenge as a practice that will broaden your bodyful experience.

1. What is an activity that you used to enjoy together that you can pick back up?
2. What is a new activity that you may be interested in inviting your partner to try with you?
3. If you already do an activity together, share with each other how you can highlight the six stages to deepen your experience of the shared experience.

6

NAVIGATING SEXUAL CHALLENGES

To share our vulnerable, precious somatic stories with an intimate partner is an opportunity to experience ourselves from a new perspective. To open the somatic self to a lover, whose touch evokes easeful pleasure-sourced movement, is a great honor and an important sensory gateway into our expansive potential. Human-connected, consensual pleasure has the potential to truly push the growing edges of our capacity—our capacity for expressive movement, our receptivity for life-affirming feelings, and our access to pleasure as a literal healing force.

To experience this with another person creates a bond that nourishes the relationship through embodied attunement, which, in turn, further nourishes us as individuals.

But when sexual intimacy is uncomfortable or painful and desire for sex feels out of reach, this expansive potential is subverted by embarrassment, shame, and avoidance. When sexual difficulties present themselves, the nervous system can dysregulate, setting off the alarm bells in the body. And when body architecture is disoriented like this, we apply all the coping habits and body armor to protect the self and disconnect from the discomfort.

Furthermore, there is little motivation to work on these sexual difficulties if (1) sex prior to this difficulty was already difficult, (2) you have absorbed the societal assumption that sex should be easeful and/or sex should be a particular set of energetic activities, and/or (3) you assume that sexy-time doesn't apply to you once your body begins to age or experience challenges. What if it is not your body that has to be different, but your view of sex that could benefit from a new perspective—a perspective that comes directly from your moment-to-moment felt experience?

DOI: 10.4324/9781003508984-9

Through layers of verbal and non-verbal social messaging, we get the message that the body must be in perfect working order, and we must experience 100% pleasure to be a healthy sexual being. This is simply not true, and certainly unrealistic given the myriad of life events that write their stories on our bodies as we live life and get older.

The truth is that we *can* enjoy the pleasure and connection of intimacy throughout the seasons of life. Even further, the quality of focus, the personal practices, and the dedication to discover our sexuality within each challenge nourish aliveness and equip us with personal skills to better deal with each challenge.

There is a freedom that can emerge from being in a body that does not align with the assumptions we've been given by society—a freedom to move at your own pace when you must listen to your body in real-time and acknowledge what actually feels good and life-giving. There is a freedom when you must discover, moment-to-moment, how you want to be engaged with as a sexual being who cannot follow the social rules of body idealism. The knowledge is within *you*. Knowledge to be discovered through the bodyful practices you do with yourself and in sexual connection with an intimate partner. Your intimate dynamic blossoms only when you acknowledge the present moment experience and growing edges of each of you. This is an opportunity for a genuine and heartfelt coming-out event as you set aside the beliefs that don't align with your present-moment self and beliefs that don't support your continued relational evolution.

You get to define sexual intimacy based on what genuinely feels good and nourishing to both of you as you are now.

Reproductive justice advocate Omisade Burney-Scott (2025) talks about the *sexual debuts* of an individual. Throughout our lives, we enter the gateways of different sexual expressions. Each sexual debut is a dynamic unveiling as the body reorganizes itself to integrate new experiences, new balances of hormones, and new features of relationships. These are the gateways of our maturation and evolution. Burney-Scott invites people to take her on a journey of their sexual debuts throughout their life, encouraging them to appreciate their human capacity for inspiration, tenderness, awkwardness, and full-body expression that reflects the magic and challenge of each life stage. It is an opportunity to be inspired by the resilience and creativity that lives within each debut.

Let this be an inspiration to you as well. As we discuss the challenges that arise in intimate relationships, remember that an intimacy challenge can pave the way for another sexual debut—a new version of your dynamic self, waiting to be revealed. A new version that has incorporated new opportunities for embodied pleasure.

Pleasure in intimacy is not frivolous—embodied pleasure (pleasure that is experienced and expressed consciously) is a healing and connecting force of the body, and it is worth the energy to find it and embrace it. Discovering pleasure while navigating a body challenge has the power to fuel your transformation. When pleasure is found and settled into during a physical difficulty, a learning (vs. defending) pre-effort state is engaged, awakening those deeper brain structures and nervous system pathways to reopen the range of possible movement and emotional options. We cannot rely on old habits—if we try to do things like we used to with a body that is different, it can feel rigid, forced, and inflexible, creating frustration and further discomfort. The commitment to discover pleasure during a body challenge becomes a radical acceptance of change—a process of grieving what was, celebrating what is accessible, and sequencing movement from the possibility found within.

And because we are social beings, pleasure within an intimate relationship has the ability to remodel your relationship patterns to be more representative of your truth while making space for your growth as you continue on the path of life together.

When Life Events Impact the Body: My Story

When I had my daughter by C-section at 31 weeks, I knew that my body would be substantially different. At that time, I focused more on my newborn and her health and well-being than my own. While I had little moments of self-care to support myself in order to better support her, I knew my larger healing work would be delayed. My healing went okay, but it took me a few years to feel strong in my body again.

When I was diagnosed with breast cancer in my early 40s, I knew that my connection with my body, with pleasure, with my partner, would be altered forever. I dedicated myself to studying this progression of surgery and recovery, applying my own clinical work to my personal experience as I entered into a sexual debut that I did not choose but would face with eyes wide open. I vowed to stay close to my body through every moment of the journey.

There was a period of time when I just could not sequence movement through my upper body at all, and the restriction created a unique challenge of figuring out how to move in daily activities and also how to move with my emotions and soften into affectionate contact. I practiced patience with the strange sensations—lightning strikes and rushing waves of nerves awakening—that would come and go through my chest, and I learned to stay afloat in the deep dance of tissues mending as my body was actively regrowing tissue, reconnecting nerves, and becoming more wholly alive. Though my body felt unknown to me, I practiced stillness and quiet, the small dance of micromovements with my awareness pressing into my somatic landscape, to hear the murmurings of familiarity and the openings of new somatic possibility. Instead of minimizing my access to pleasure or distancing from my somatic self, I found renewed and expanded capacity for life. I discovered that *pleasure literally heals the body*. My surgeons shared with me how impressed they were with my healing process and encouraged me to share my experience with others.

With my committed partner alongside me, our relationship and attunement with each other deepened. Our intimacy broadened and became more satisfying than ever. Through this exploration, my intimate partner also discovered new aspects of himself, deeper access to expanding his senses, and an expanded ability to hold a wider range of emotions as he found attunement with himself and with me. My health challenge became an invitation for both of us to slow our awareness in shared moments that had previously been rather easeful to find new pathways of pleasure that took into account the changes in my body topography. We could not take anything for granted, and this created a more intentional connection between us.

I would not take back this experience for anything.

Now, as I navigate perimenopause, I continue to apply the principles and practices that I share in this chapter to reframe difficulties as challenges and gateways into opportunity to celebrate the majesty of this resilient human body.

Embracing Differences as Fuel for Evolution

Just as in my experience, there are many types of challenges that emerge during intimate relationships that create a difference in how you experience intimacy and how you understand your body and the body of your partner. Body differences such as health and medical challenges, hormone shifts, pregnancy, neurodivergence, arousal non-concordance, asexuality, and disability can all impact how physical and sexual intimacy are experienced. This can be a source of misunderstanding and difficulty, so we will explore several of these challenges to give you a sense of the particular features of these differences, as well as how to reframe them from a problem that you suffer from to a challenge that you can navigate to fuel a deeper connection.

Fundamentally, the most normal and natural feature of being in a human body is that we all have differences and that the body changes over time. This is not a problem, this is normal, and it is an opportunity.

Arousal Non-Concordance

Arousal non-concordance (Nagoski, 2015) is an inner experience of feeling two seemingly opposing feelings about sensual/sexual experience at the same time. Perhaps your mind and your heart are interested in sexual intimacy, but your arousal anatomy is not coming online—you are feeling emotionally connected with your partner and have the time for intimacy, but your arousal anatomy is unaroused as you begin touching and connecting physically. Or your arousal anatomy is activated while your mind and heart are not interested in engaging sexually—your arousal anatomy is already expanding and responding, but you are still feeling hurt by something your partner said, or you are feeling anxious because you are late to work. Think of this as feeling both yes and no in the body at the same time. This is incredibly normal and a common experience as we move through the variability of life.

It is tempting—and the go-to for many people—to override the inner feeling of no when you are prioritizing the relationship, wanting to "keep the peace," or are in the habit of disregarding your discomfort. It is a feature of socialization that we suppress our own comfort, needs, or desires to align with the standards of engagement. This internal override begins when the parent tells the child to "hug your grandparent" when they don't feel comfortable, but the child feels compelled to do it anyway. When you sit in your manager's office as they give you a duty to do that you loathe. When you attend your first gynecology or urology appointment, and they bluntly instruct you through a medical exam of your central arousal anatomy. Being told by a parent or a pastor that exploring your body is to be avoided. Combine this social mechanism of suppressing discomfort with the ideals of what sex is *supposed* to look and feel like, and we have a recipe for arousal non-concordance and performance-based (not pleasure-based) sex or sexual avoidance.

Arousal non-concordance in intimate relationships can be identified in different forms. As I list some of the sources, make notes about which you identify with and which you think your partner may identify with. This list is not exhaustive, but hopefully gives you an idea of possible sources:

- **Cognitive source of arousal non-concordance**: Intrusive and distracting thoughts (such as *Did I change over the laundry? Will the kids burst in? What do I look like right now? I need to finish that project!*), a misunderstanding or lack of information about the activities involved in sex, an assumption about what your partner desires, or overstimulation from incoming sensory information.
- **Emotional source of arousal non-concordance**: Feeling hurt by something your partner said or did, feeling emotionally disconnected from your partner, feeling anxious or distraught about a life situation, or general emotional dysregulation.
- **Physical source of arousal non-concordance**: Physical pain, sex triggering or exasperating genital infections, exhaustion, suppression of arousal anatomy response due to medication, surgery, injury, or hormonal shifts.
- **Somatic source of arousal non-concordance**: You and your partner's bodies moving at a different pace or rhythm, body memories of trauma surfacing, feeling uncomfortable in the space when the immediate environment is not aesthetically resonating with your nervous system (i.e., the room is messy, cold).

Whatever the source of arousal non-concordance is, notice how your arousal anatomy is intricately linked with your broader nervous system. Being able to identify the source of the arousal non-concordance helps you to identify the gateway into your body—the place to begin a somatic creative process of embodied intimacy. Embodied intimacy invites you to slow down around the no's to support what your body needs for genuine intimacy. Overriding the no will further disconnect you from your body—both the uncomfortable feelings and the pleasurable feelings—as your body doubles down on a lack of trust in human connection, building resentment over time.

This no is here for a reason—putting on the brakes, as sex educator Emily Nagoski (2015) would say—to stop you from accelerating forward and leaving something important behind, or walking into a situation that your body fears may not be a good experience. Remember that *someone else's arousal is not more important than your comfort.* Validate that your body is feeling this for a reason, and once you determine what might be helpful in softening the no without force, you have something to request or advocate for. If it is as simple as "did I change over the laundry?," why not just go and check? Once the laundry is put in the dryer, check in with that feeling again—is it the same or different? If it softened, ask yourself if a no for intimacy is still true. It is possible that you may feel more congruent in yourself and more open and interested in intimacy.

When it is a cognitive source, slow down and identify the intrusive thought or distracting thought pattern that is showing up as a no in this moment. Dislodge your attention from the thought and check in with your body. Begin by checking in with your breath—you may find that you are breathing quite shallow and that your chest feels constricted. Ask this shallow breath and constricted chest feeling what it wants you to know, thank it for trying to protect you, and ask the feeling what it needs to soften so you can land more fully in this moment. Then make a request to resolve what is needed.

When the source of the no in arousal non-concordance is something a bit more complex, such as having hurt feelings toward your intimate partner, you will need a bit more time and more involvement from your partner. Share your feeling with your partner: "I notice that my heart feels achy remembering when you said x,y,z yesterday." Partner, you then get to own the impact, not necessarily the intention, that your words or actions had on your partner. If it was hurtful to them, it probably has roots in their childhood, a prior relationship, or earlier in your relationship with them. Tell them *what makes sense* about why what you said was hurtful based on what you know is important to your partner. Tell them, "That makes sense because I know that topic is tender for you." There is a relief that comes from not having to defend a feeling. Instead of putting energy into defenses, they can put energy into connection, thank you for acknowledging their hurt, and begin to soften into intimacy.

When arousal non-concordance is from a physical source, this is an opportunity to directly re-pattern your sexual paradigm to a more real-time way of relating to your body, the body of your partner, and sexuality in general. For example, if you are anticipating feeling discomfort or pain, talk with your partner about your concern, take expectations off the table, and explore together what might be helpful—slowing down, relaxing first, beginning with stillness/attunement touch or massage, and so on. I'll talk more about this in the next section.

When arousal non-concordance is from a somatic source, you get to explore more about your embodied expression and learn to move at the pace of your connection with yourselves and your attunement with each other. Chapter 9, *The Rhythms of Intimacy*, will discuss somatic attunement in depth.

Here, trauma body memories have an opportunity to begin to heal when you are able to acknowledge the resulting body dysregulation, be supported by your partner, and return to intimacy when an inner yes appears.

If the environment is not feeling aesthetically supportive to attending to your inner experience and pleasurable contact, consider what types of environments support sensuality and present-moment awareness. Craft your environment to support this more bodyful kind of presence.

Some partners feel hurt if their partner expresses arousal non-concordance during intimacy. They report feeling unwanted or fear that their partner doesn't actually feel desire for them. Learning how normal arousal non-concordance is, and that it has less to do with a partner's attraction and more to do with the way the nervous system shifts between states, can soften hurt feelings. Consider helping your partner complete something, or make the space more comfortable when they are distracted or fearful. Use arousal non-concordance as an opportunity to connect emotionally and strengthen your sense of partnership with each other.

Intimacy Challenges Due to Health and Medical Events

Health and medical issues create a collection of challenges for intimate partners. Like so many loose strings on a tapestry, it can feel overwhelming to determine which to pull and reweave into your life first. Do I focus on getting my diet in order first, or should I start with therapy and mental health? Do I do consultations with a neurologist or an endocrinologist first to work on balancing my symptoms? Do we use a babysitter for our medical appointments or for relaxation and date time? It can be a maze of options, and each route can feel like a full-time job to investigate and build new practices and habits. So, prioritizing your intimacy while navigating challenging body issues can feel overwhelming.

One confounding challenge is that the dominant social narrative ties sexuality and sexiness to an "ideal" body type and ability, so when the body experiences medical challenges, such as recovering from surgery, pregnancy, or going through perimenopause or andropause, sex can feel hopelessly unsatisfying—especially when we are wired to expect sex to happen in a particular way.

This isn't just in your mind. Your nervous system and muscles hold memories—both in your endogenous body rhythms of organ systems and in motor plans of the somatic nervous system that help us to anticipate how the body should respond to certain stimuli and situations. Notice how you have consistent motor plans for many situations. For example, you probably hold your partner's hand the same way most times, you probably have your preferred bedtime routine and position that you nestle into for sleep, and you and your partner have probably developed your routines for sex. In other words, we optimize our activities to use a reasonable amount of energy for the best results. When body changes happen, our tried-and-true motor plans become ineffective or even impossible.

Health and medical challenges can create bodily discomfort that can be prohibitive to engage in intimacy as you formerly knew it. Whether it is physical pain, bloating, or brain fog, these challenges don't let you start intimacy in a familiar way, which can create an immediate roadblock. Meeting a roadblock at the start of intimacy flies in the face of the idea that arousal should pick you up and erase any barriers, so you may think, *well, I guess sex isn't for me right now.*

Actually, this is another golden opportunity to redefine sex, discover pleasure in new ways, somatically rewrite old and ineffective erotic patterns, and assist your body in healing well. You get to explore what activities, qualities of touch and breath, and what forms of movement help you feel a little less discomfort, a little less pain, so you can follow the somatic discovery to a new way of embodiment and pleasure.

When sexual energy does not flow as easily, or your momentum of arousal does not work the way it did previously, the inner aliveness and creativity of sexual energy can encourage you to develop a deeper relationship with your somatic self. This is a time to find new pathways to provide emotional and physiological healing.

When you or a partner is struck with a medical issue such as cancer, surgery, an autoimmune disease, and so on, you begin a journey that fundamentally shifts how you experience your body, your sexuality, and the meaning of life itself—it's an existential earthquake. Your intimate relationship will feel this earthquake, forcing you to reconsider aspects of your sex life that were working just fine, as well as the aspects that haven't felt great for a while.

Understanding sexuality as a life-giving flow of energy throughout the body, it makes sense that it will get snagged or clogged up when something medical is amiss. Disease and illness create interruptions, stagnation, and inflammation in healthy cells and tissues—an understandable bodily response to the stress and environmental toxins of the modern world. Your body is not failing you—it's just that the world is too big for us to handle at times, and your body cannot keep up. While sexuality is a life-giving energy, medical issues feel like life-draining complications.

This interruption to the flow of sexual energy can emerge in many ways throughout your somatic landscape. Perhaps your heart medication makes erections less likely to happen or last as long as you would like, or perhaps the scars forming after surgery have interrupted the sensation in that area of your body so that what was once pleasurable now feels numb or unpleasant (this will change over time as the brilliant nerve systems rewire themselves).

If you are experiencing an autoimmune disease, the myriad of symptoms can feel overwhelming, and you have probably spent a fair amount of time just trying to get an accurate diagnosis. This is an all-consuming journey, a continually moving target that comes with a process of elimination (of food, activity, household chemical products, etc.) to discover the right path forward.

Perhaps you are receiving rounds of radiation or chemotherapy and experiencing the side effects such as fatigue, nausea, digestive issues, skin changes, weight loss, and mood changes. All of these things will impact your libido and change your experience of arousal and desire. However, "few cancer treatments (other than those affecting some area of the brain or spinal cord) damage the nerves and muscles involved in feeling pleasure from touch and reaching orgasm (American Cancer Society, Shover, 15)," which means that while it may be different, pleasure can still be a part of your life and relationships.

When your life feels threatened by cancer or disrupted and overwhelmed by managing other illnesses and chronic medical issues, it can feel like a stretch to devote time to pleasure-based connection with yourself and with an intimate partner. Determining what feels good or what is supportive and nourishing to your body can feel like a losing battle. It is incredibly disheartening when many of your former resources and happy places don't feel good, as you are overwhelmed by uncomfortable or painful sensations. Your happy places may now be tinged with fear, frustration, heaviness, and a feeling of being deeply unsatisfied. It is very difficult to find a place of yield and buoyant flow when your body, the vessel that takes you everywhere, is suffering emotionally, physically, and existentially.

As I have said, pleasure is literally healing to the body. Pleasure increases fresh blood and oxygen to affected areas of the body, it eases stress and releases feel-good neurochemicals and hormones, and it directs your body to life-giving pathways of movement and expression. When your go-to pleasurable activities aren't accessible, don't give up! Widening your options for pleasure without any expectations of what is supposed to happen or what a partner expects allows you to discover new options, new resources for you to call on when things feel challenging.

However frightening and terribly inconvenient, this earthquake and the proceeding search for pleasure offer an opportunity to awaken the deeper brain structures that hold your somatic and relational patterns—patterns that are created earlier in life—by following the threads of pleasure as they are discovered. When your body cannot move or respond in the way that is expected, the brain and body itself need to accommodate the changes. For a period of time or longer, you cannot take for granted your ability to walk, take a shower, and touch and hold an intimate partner, among other daily activities. You are now compelled to slow down and get creative. Instead of the tried-and-true muscle coordination patterns, you begin to focus all your attention on the present moment in order to *move at the pace of your body.* The deeper brain structures, such as the orbital-medial prefrontal cortex, which is deeply intertwined with the limbic brain (the emotion and memory center of the brain), activate with this kind of attention. You are compelled to adjust your movement to experience a little less pain, and perhaps relief and even pleasure, as you find the openings in your movement to complete a task, move from point A to point B, or follow your desire for loving contact. This opens the brain and nervous system to rewiring itself—an opportunity to develop an increased inner somatic awareness, more effective and satisfying relational patterns, and a more friendly connection with the body.

You will learn that, yes, you can notice an inner desire for movement, you can follow it, and you receive a positive response. This moment-to-moment dance of gathering up your body integration and following movement impulse with breath support is the foundation of a fully embodied expression in relationship, regardless of your body ability.

Adding this somatic creative process to your daily life is hugely beneficial in between treatments, or once the medical treatment is done and recovery is happening, as you may find yourself just trying to get back to life as normal, only to discover that things are different. Your body is not the same. You may experience fear or anxiety that sexual activity, including intercourse, will be painful and that your body may not respond the way it used to—perhaps you'll have difficulty with body discomfort, erection, lubrication, or orgasm.

It may feel challenging to find attunement with your own body when you experience the uncertainty that comes with medical challenges. It is also difficult to attune with your partner when you are not the one experiencing the body reorganization. But prioritizing partner intimacy is a way to reconnect in the midst of challenge, experience life-affirming moments, and also repattern the ineffective and unsatisfying components of your connection.

Bringing attention to the present moment and following new movement impulses opens your capability for more full and genuine expression. Allow your emotions to move with your physical movement. *Sometimes your body just needs to cry.* Invite the tears, the frustration, and other emergent emotions to instruct you on how you need to move to find release, allowing the rest of your body to soften around the feeling. After you have followed the movement, rest for a moment in an active—awake and dedicated—yield to notice if the emotion feels the same or different. This is the somatic creative process where your partner can join you when you feel ready so that you can learn to do this practice together, offering the opportunity to attune body-to-body.

For the partner who took care of their intimate other during their medical event, intentionally transitioning back from caregiver to lover is an important and life-affirming part of the journey that often gets overlooked. You have witnessed the suffering of your partner, their brave journey back to living life, and all the emotions, awkwardness, and messiness that come with it. You cannot just go back to the way it was. Once the body has a profound experience, you are forever changed in both small and large ways. The relationship dynamic is also deeply impacted.

As the partner, you first transition from intimate partner and lover to caregiver and household-runner as your partner goes through treatment and into recovery. You develop caregiver/care-receiver patterns that become built into your connection by necessity that later you find are still present and perhaps very unsexy. Caregivers often set aside their own needs and desires during interactions with the person they are caring for, which is a reasonable response when someone is in need of daily support. Suppressing your own desires in the presence of an intimate partner stalls the momentum of arousal—the beginning of the dance, when continually interrupted, over time can lose its compelling pathway toward intimate engagement. This momentum of arousal can be reclaimed through an attuning somatic practice that I will share in the third section.

You also have new knowledge and awareness from the care dynamic that becomes valuable to your relationship going forward. Caring for your intimate partner and receiving care is an expression of love that can deepen a bond. Together, you practice deep listening to what is needed when the body is in great need. There is a tenderness that can emerge from this deep listening that you can carry forward into the rest of your relationship. This deep listening and attunement, when combined with a mutual experience of pleasure, can increase intimate satisfaction.

In addition, priorities in caring for the home can shift and expand as one person rests and the other takes on more responsibility and calls in their family and community to help. In taking on more responsibilities in the home, the caregiving partner will be compelled to seek more support of their own, deepening their resource pool as they connect with family, friends, exercise, a therapist, and so on. When the caregiver receives their own support, they have more energy to offer support. This process can highlight how to better distribute household responsibilities going forward, supporting more energy conservation and allowing more energy and appreciation of each other to support intimacy.

As you transition back into sexual intimacy, notice what patterns of relating in the care dynamic feel important to take with you:

- Greater kindness and patience
- Embracing a wider range of emotional experience and expression
- Greater appreciation for the body and for your relationship based on learning what you can endure and accomplish together
- Investing in attunement, slowing down to feel the somatic experience and move at the pace of connection
- Interest in each other's experience
- Finding the value in engaging in support and activities that are important to your personal aliveness
- Better, more detailed communication
- A greater sense of teamwork

Also, notice what relational patterns from the care dynamic need to be let go:

- Suppressing feelings and desires
- Inequity in the management of the home
- Seeing a partner as unable to care for themselves
- Releasing movements toward each other that come from expectation or functional care

Once the immediacy of a medical issue has passed, or the medical issue is now a continued part of life, and getting to a new normal is the focus, it is time to create life-affirming environments, both physical and relational, to integrate the wisdom of the healing process. Investing in another sexuality debut encourages your relationship to be infused with aliveness.

7

SEXUALITY CHALLENGES DUE TO HORMONE-RELATED LIFE EVENTS AND TRANSITIONS

The shifts and changes of hormones throughout your lifespan create a broad landscape of impact on your body, your emotions, and your intimacy. Hormones support so many body systems that when pregnancy, menopause, andropause, and other endocrine-centric events emerge, tending to your body is central to rediscovering your vitality and balance. Women's health expert Dr. Aviva Romm (2021) reminds us that "while the medical model treats us otherwise, you are not a bunch of unrelated parts stuck together. You're a whole person, and every aspect of your life influences your hormonal health (Romm, 4)." Romm encourages her patients and readers to see the symptoms of hormonal changes as "vital signs offering you powerful information that act as a compass, a complete *inner guidance system* (Romm, 6)" that you can learn to validate and rely on for information about what you need.

Since I am not a medical doctor, I have gathered information from a few of the foremost experts on hormone-related life events, and I present a few major milestones for you to consider how they impact your body and your relationship. I encourage you to talk with appropriate health professionals about the material presented here—this chapter can be a great jumping-off point to start a potential challenging conversation with a partner or a health provider.

Let's explore three hormone-related events that are opportunities to deepen your connection with your body and to transform your intimate relationship.

Pregnancy

One of the great challenges to a couple's intimacy is pregnancy, pregnancy loss, childbirth, and the period of time when your child is growing

DOI: 10.4324/9781003508984-10

from infancy until kindergarten. Psychotherapist and author Esther Perel (2007) said that love and attraction make babies, which then spells erotic disaster for the parents. Bringing a child into the world reorganizes absolutely everything! From your identity, to your body, to your schedule, to your emotional capacity, and to your relationship priorities, pregnancy impacts all corners of your experience in both challenging and life-affirming ways.

Between the dramatic changes in hormones, the reorganization of your body during and after pregnancy, the lack of sleep, and the shifting of priorities to fully caring for an infant, getting back to sex as it was after six weeks is not always possible. Getting back to moments of intimacy, however, is an important and meaningful gateway back into yourself as an individual—not just a parent who tends to the needs of your infant—and a gateway back into your connection as a couple. This learning gets woven into the whole of who you are now that you are cultivating the health of your family.

Regardless of the method of delivery, the structure of the pelvis is different after pregnancy, and your relationship with your magnificent body is forever changed. First of all, realizing that you can get pregnant is a life-changing revelation. After pregnancy, you are healing from stretched or torn tissues and the pelvic bones coming back together after expanding, incisions, scar tissue from tearing or episiotomy or cesarean, muscle pain and soreness, fatigue, and hormones that are trying to rebalance, causing mood changes and changes to your arousal anatomy. You may experience an increase in anxiety or depression during this period, so the intimacy that you engage in with a partner must honor this immense journey that you have been through—both the emotional journey and the somatic body story.

When you and your partner honor the body both during and after pregnancy, creating a welcoming environment for all the ways that you are impacted, you pave the way for whole-body healing, greater attunement with each other, and a deeper level of intimacy feeding your intimacy during this time not only creates a deeper connection for you to enjoy but also offers a model for your children on how to be in an embodied relationship.

Also, you may find that the shift in roles within the relationship can be quite shocking. Even if you intellectually understand that your attention will be on the baby and you will be working as a team instead of focusing on each other, the reality of how this feels in the body can activate challenging feelings toward each other. You are carrying an emotional complexity that is difficult to reconcile—of course, both of your attention is on the baby, other children you may have, and running the household, yet at the same time, it can be hurtful to feel your partner's attention focused away from you and the ways that you used to look to each other for connection. You don't stop having needs or desires during this period; in fact, these needs and desires will feel heightened at times. You will begin to long for the opportunity to move at your own rhythm instead of constantly moving at the rhythm of those who need you.

It is at this point that you get to begin to reinvest in connection with each other, expanding the repertoire of how you share intimate moments. While you may receive an abundance of touch with your infant and children, you are not receiving the grounded and intentional quality of *adult touch*. This is where you can initially focus your intention—learning what kinds of adult touch help your body to feel rooted, relaxed, and attuned. When you spend most of your time attuning to the needs and playful connection with your little one, your energy can be replenished by having your partner attune to you. Sharing the Bodyful Touch Practice found in Chapter 11 begins to establish a rhythm of engaging and communicating about what kind of adult touch feels personally resourcing and relationally connecting. Perhaps you begin by having a few moments on the couch or in bed to massage each other's hands. Or perhaps you take a walk together alone or with your little one in a stroller or baby wrap carrier, where you can have emotional and physical contact with each other, sharing affection and gratitude.

This is a season of life. Broaden your repertoire of options for connection, so you can carry a broader skillset for the natural changes that come as little ones get older and your personal time begins to increase again.

Perimenopause and Menopause

Perimenopause precedes menopause when your reproductive capacity is winding down. The ovaries release their last collection of eggs in uneven intervals, and the brain modulates the body's response to fluctuations in estrogen, specifically estradiol. This creates changes in your brain and body—a brilliant, albeit uncomfortable, remodeling of your physiological architecture to adapt to the next life stage. As the brain and body shift the type of estrogen used, from estradiol to estrone, you are being neurobiologically reorganized to address the set of tasks and life focus that you are transitioning into. This can happen over a period of about ten years, or it can be sudden due to medical or surgical procedures (oophorectomy, chemotherapy, tamoxifen, etc.) or initiated as a component of gender-affirming care. Instead of the body organizing itself to support a potential pregnancy, it shifts its orientation to channel that generative energy elsewhere.

As the ovaries start unreliably producing estradiol, a system-wide reorganization starts setting off all kinds of alarm bells and producing an absolute fiasco of symptoms. Once menopause fully arrives—when you haven't menstruated in a full 365 days—another form of estrogen, estrone, has fully taken the place of estradiol, and the body will begin to stabilize. This is a transition that all women and estrogen-dominant people will experience.

Losing estradiol is no small matter. Neuroscientist and researcher Dr. Lisa Mosconi (2024) calls estradiol the "CEO of the female brain." It manages and supports a whole landscape of important and interconnected processes: it is a neuroprotector, protecting the brain and brain function; it boosts the immune system; it supports new cell growth and supports the brain to adapt to changes; it supports serotonin, the neurotransmitter that promotes happiness and pleasure; it protects the brain from oxidative stress; it supports blood pressure and circulation and protects against vascular damage; and it manages efficient use of glucose for energy.

During perimenopause, as your ovaries begin to abruptly start and stop estradiol production, you are literally losing gray matter in the brain, and brain energy activity is diminished. While the cognitive challenges of this time do not put you in the "impaired" range—research has shown that menopausal women still outperform men on some cognitive tests—it can feel like you are losing your mind as your emotions are more sensitive and harder to regulate, you can't focus as well or remember particular details, you can't multitask as easily as you used to, and it's harder to follow the flow of conversation.

Physically, you can experience hot flashes as your hypothalamus can't regulate temperature as well, and you can experience joint pain, vaginal atrophy and dryness, breast soreness, heart palpitations, digestive issues, thinning hair, body odor changes, hearing changes, new allergies, fatigue, and sleep disturbances.

Emotionally, you can experience an increase in anxiety and depressed mood. If you've never struggled with anxiety or depression, this may be the first time that you do. And if you have had difficulties with this in the past, it can worsen during perimenopause. This emotional upheaval is not for nothing. This is a time to allow your heart to grieve what is being lost so that you can prepare and look forward to what you will gain. Your fluctuating emotions become guideposts to slow down, to let the tears fall, to let the anxiety guide your body to move in a supportive way that meets its intensity, and to take the day off to rest.

Perimenopause also causes body fat to redistribute. As the body is going through estradiol withdrawal, more estrone is created to bring support and balance. Estrone is created in adipose tissue (fat tissue), especially around the middle of the body, so the body creates more to provide the needed reserves. This increase in fat tissue can provoke the body criticism so prevalent in society and, due to our social nature, woven so deeply into our experience of ourselves and sense of sexiness. This is one reason perimenopausal people can struggle with negative self-image and may begin to avoid intimate activity. I encourage my clients to make sure that they get movement and exercise that they truly enjoy and give love to their bellies instead of focusing on "melting belly fat" as so many shame-inducing advertisements tout. We benefit from a little more belly fat during this time to support the body in reorganizing how estrogen is used in the body.

According to Dr. Mosconi, "historically perceived in the extreme negative, menopause comes with the stigmas associated with ageism, the demise of one's vitality, and even the end of our identity as women" (Mosconi, 2024, 5). The lack of research on this incredibly important life transition is astounding, since menstruating people make up half of the population and will spend about 40% of their lifespan in menopause. Dr. Mosconi asserts that "out of sheer numbers alone, menopause should be a major sociocultural event and the subject of extensive investigation and deep knowledge" (Mosconi, 5).

Like sex, perimenopause suffers from a culture that doesn't prioritize its monumental life transition importance or capitalize on the industry of preventing the natural impact. Professor, author, and activist Heather Corinna says that the history itself of menopause has "mostly been written and codified by people it's personally enriched who couldn't even themselves experience menopause in the first place. It's been exploitive, abusive, violent, and sometimes even fatal" (Corinna, 2021, 24). Unfortunately, the dominant culture and a wide swath of the medical professional community don't receive training in menopause and therefore either perpetuate misinformation or resort to simply addressing the symptoms. This is beginning to change, which is a relief, but we have a long way to go. The truth is that menopause is not something that just happens, and you just have to get through it. The recent flood of social media content—both comedic and informational—is beginning to generate a broader perspective of menopause and the importance of embracing the process. There is actually a lot that can be done to make this transition more easeful and community support that can make it more meaningful.

Due to misinformation and a limited amount of research, lack of informed intimacy skills, and underlying relational wounds, this transformational stage often reveals or exacerbates relationship challenges. It can be truly destabilizing! Libido can fluctuate widely or flatline during this time, vaginal dryness and atrophy can make central arousal anatomy contact painful, digestive issues and bloating can make closeness uncomfortable, and fatigue and decreased ability to manage stress can leave far less energy to dedicate to navigating intimacy in a body that is already running on lower energy stores. In addition, your attitude toward sex before menopause is linked to your attitude after menopause. A satisfying physical and emotional relationship to sex predicted higher importance during perimenopause and menopause, according to the *Study of Women's Health Across the Nation (SWAN)*, a longitudinal study of 3,302 women (Sutton-Tyrrell et al., 2018).

While this time has been disregarded and vilified, it is actually a valuable time of reclamation and opportunity. Far from being irrelevant and non-sexual, perimenopausal and post-menopausal people have a valuable intimate perspective and can enjoy a broader, richer view of eroticism.

If your emotions didn't demand your attention, would you take the time to honor this immense transition from a body that can create life to a body that has more energy and focus to pass on wisdom with a broader palette of creativity? This is the wisdom of the menopausal transition.

Slowing down to track this journey, you will notice that these symptoms come in cycles, which can be difficult to predict as progesterone decreases and estradiol production tanks for a period of time and then lurches back.

As you read this section together (and I recommend that you read it together! Your non-menopausal partner will benefit from understanding your experience to make a team out of this monumental life transition), make note of what is showing up for you in terms of symptoms. Also, make note of what is important to your body, heart, and intimacy during this life stage—what do you prioritize or want to prioritize, what do you miss about your younger years that you are letting go of, and what are you inviting to come with you, and what are you looking forward to in your second half of life. You get to learn together! This is an important first step of deepening your communication in intimate spaces, making adjustments to your sexy-time that supports this seismic shift that is happening. Make agreements with each other that you will invest more in erotic gateways for their own sake and enjoyment, that you will slow down and explore what is needed moment to moment to support the perimenopausal body and heart (more kind words, more massage, more embodied communication, a better personal lubricant, and a slower pace). You can also track your changing menstrual and hormonal cycle together, so that both of you are on the same page about what is happening in the body and what might be needed at different stages.

Recognize the superpower that you are developing during this transition. Post-menopause brings greater discernment, more balance, a deeper self-knowing, and the potential to develop a broader palette of intimacy since the reorganization of perimenopause opens you to a realm of new possibilities and detachment from old, unrealistic expectations. This is the benefit of having an intentional focus within a pre-effort (uncoordinated and learning) stage of life (see Chapter 2)—you get to notice when the moments of full-effort expression appear, moments where you recognize yourself again and see glimpses of who you are becoming.

Tending to the body and your intimate relationship well during perimenopause sets you up for a more fulfilling second half of life. Once you start growing more gray matter on top of the new brain organization post-menopause (one of the few times in your life that you actually grow more brain tissue in adulthood), you get to build on the new learning you have acquired about what truly supports your body and investing in what is truly meaningful and nourishing to you and your relationships. Due to the seismic shifts within your body, your very instincts begin to change.

Instead of adding one more duty at work, you delegate in order to keep your exercise or rest time because you know that you burn out faster. Instead of signing up for one more community role, you decide to invest more in the meaningful roles that you already hold. Instead of forcing your body into uncomfortable clothing, you ask a friend or stylist to help you explore a wardrobe style that is more comfortable and better suits you now. And instead of saying yes to the kind of sex that you don't enjoy, you invite your intimate partner to join you in an erotic gateway that supports your body to relax and suggest a way of engaging in sexy-time that genuinely feels good to you, which also provides an opportunity for your partner to learn something new about themselves. Your body is inviting (i.e., directly telling you) to invest in what is actually a priority for you. Learn what your capacity *actually* is at this time. You will need more restorative time, and that is a good thing. It makes more time for the spark of creativity, time to savor the moment, and invite more pleasure into your life.

We also need more movement during this time. Movement and exercise support the interwoven processes of the body, and it reduces stress, anxiety, and depression. When you are doing your daily yoga practice, riding your bike, weightlifting, or dancing, connect with the emotions in your body to encourage them to move you. Emotions that get met with internally sequenced *motion* (embodied motion) get to express and become what is next—relief, tears, lightness, softening, and laughter. When emotions are moved with the muscles and tissues of the body, they get unstuck, and they inform you about what you are truly needing for your aliveness. Connecting emotion with movement heals in-the-moment discomfort as well as old trauma on a deeper level through a somatic creative process that we will explore in the next section.

This phase of life matters. What you focus on now and how you connect with your body gets woven into your new brain–body organization. When you receive support through this major life transformation from yourself, your family, and your healthcare team, you can better manage the more extreme symptoms of perimenopause.

Your healthcare team (naturopath, nutritionist, primary care physician, gynecologist, Chinese medicine doctor, personal trainer, etc.) can offer support in the form of a change in nutrition, exercise, supplements, and can let you know if you are a good candidate for hormone replacement therapy (HRT). Don't just muscle through it—this is an opportunity to receive support and do menopause *well* so that you can share your creativity and wisdom with the world.

Sexuality is the movement of your creative, generative energy, and it is shifting pathways during perimenopause. When you practice secure attachment with your body through these frustrating changes, you can rewire your relationship with your whole self. You may experience a renewed feeling of desire and interest in intimacy, especially in the late postmenopausal stage (Sutton-Tyrrell et al., 2018).

Engage in intentional relationship to pleasure of all kinds and slow down, following genuine desire in the moment. Be open to being surprised!

Andropause

Andropause is referred to as "male menopause" and occurs in most men, though it is not a universal experience (some men maintain higher testosterone levels into older age). Instead of the seismic hormonal shifts of the estrogen-based menopause, andropause is a gradual reduction in testosterone beginning around age 40 years for men or initiated as a part of gender-affirming care. Even though it is a gradual process, andropause can cause uncomfortable body symptoms that affect your experience of your body and your intimacy with a partner.

Testosterone is the motivator hormone. It gets you going and supports lean muscle production, bone density, mood regulation, red blood cell production, energy, and mental focus. With the gradual reduction in testosterone, you may experience more fatigue, mood challenges such as low mood or anxiousness, less muscle mass and an increase in body fat, and less consistent sexual function with a lower libido and less reliable erections.

In a culture that emphasizes virility in men, declining testosterone can bring with it feelings of losing one's identity as a man, feeling less masculine, and an increased judgment over the sexual function or responsiveness of one's arousal anatomy. You may start to feel alone and alienated when you feel like your body is starting to not fit the ideal that you see in magazines, movies (Wolverine, anyone?), or at the gym. When you combine these feelings with very real physical challenges and a culture that socializes men to not talk about their feelings or show vulnerability, you have a recipe for a disorienting discontent within yourself and erotic disconnection from an intimate partner. As with other aspects of sexuality, the lack of information and misleading social messages can cause your frustration to come out sideways.

In a 2025 study of the impact of andropause on employed Japanese men (Tanji, Kawajiri, etc.), researchers found that the daily lives of men were significantly impacted by moderate to severe symptoms of andropause. This impact was most notable in work and social relationships, where they theorize that maintenance of the masculine image is most prominent. The researchers believe that:

> *This may partly reflect enduring concepts of "masculinity," despite progress toward gender equality. Masculinity involves traits such as*

> *self-reliance, stoicism, strength, and toughness, and men often strive to appear strong in social contexts. In addition, testosterone functions as a social hormone, influencing motivation, risk-taking, and competitiveness. Its levels have been shown to rise in response to social recognition. These background factors may lead men to maintain their usual work performance, even while experiencing andropause symptoms, which could in turn increase their sense of burden.*

This shift into creating less testosterone is an opportunity to incorporate better self-care into your daily life, increase your social connections, broaden the palette of how you experience pleasure and sex, and define masculinity for yourself.

This is a process that may be unfamiliar to you, since the culture does not necessarily support men to do personal evolution work or give spaces to explore themselves. You can begin to discern how your expression of masculinity supports your aliveness, supports your role in relationships that create satisfying connections, and elevates your ability to enjoy meaningful pursuits; you can also discern how your expression of masculinity has been life-draining (while validating how it has served you within certain contexts), how your expression has been life-affirming, and investing your energy in the more life-affirming ways. With lower levels of testosterone, you can learn to invest your energy in the ways of being that increase your energy, effectiveness, and enjoyment of life. Similar to menopause, andropause encourages you to shift your creative energy into broadening your base of life-affirming activities.

In terms of pleasure and sex, andropause encourages you to explore the pleasure potential of your *whole* body to support the activation of your arousal anatomy when erections are not as quick to happen or as consistent to maintain as they were in your younger life. When the immediacy and accelerated momentum of arousal happens with less frequency or slower momentum, movement toward pleasure takes on a different dimension. It allows you to relax more into the present moment, softens the momentum toward orgasm, and can reveal spaces to yield into savoring that were previously bypassed. It opens a dimension of broader somatic creativity and a potential for increased self-care. As I have talked about in other sections of this chapter, when body changes appear, other options present themselves when you dedicate yourself to looking for them.

Sharing your feelings and concerns with your partner about this process can serve to deepen your bond. Expressing your thoughts, feelings, and inspirations allows your partner to *feel* you as a three-dimensional person and refines your ability to attune with your partner somatically. Consider what you need to feel safe enough to begin this conversation, since andropause can be a difficult topic to bring up. It is not often talked about, so take your time to find the language that works for you.

Share your concerns with your healthcare team so that they can recommend lifestyle changes related to diet, exercise, and sleep hygiene, as well as any medical interventions such as HRT or a prescription to support sexual function. Look for a local men's group to find support in the company of other men who are struggling and finding inspiration around similar challenges. If you are experiencing reduced energy and low mood, there are accessible tools that you can gather—you don't have to resign yourself to muscling through this transition.

When you dedicate time to care for your body, you open a whole world of possibilities for you and for your relationship. Perhaps you decide to begin a new physical activity to support your body and testosterone—take this opportunity to make new friends who also enjoy the activity. When changes in the body cause you to feel like you don't "fit," the loneliness that develops compounds the physical and emotional symptoms. By engaging with others in a similar life stage, you learn that you are, in fact, not alone and can even start conversations about what others are learning to better support their bodies and hearts.

You can also invite your partner to join you in a new endeavor. Allow them to see you engaging in a new activity or picking up an old one that you haven't done in years. It can be quite compelling to witness your partner exploring a new side of themselves with enthusiasm and dedication.

Is It Desire Difference, or a Difference in How Your Body Relates to Desire?

In this section, I presented a few circumstances where you and a partner may not align in your interest for intimacy due to hormones shifting, altering the body landscape that you may have once known. It is a superficial assessment to say that you and your partner have a desire difference when these body events occur. While your outward desire for intimacy may look different, the desire to connect, to have a moment of aliveness together, is very much present and beneficial to your journey and to your relationship.

The invitation here is to slow your awareness around the situation, get curious about *what kind of connection is desired,* and discern *what a body going through a change needs to connect with a feeling of desire* and the onramp to pleasurable arousal (both sexual and non-sexual). Desire is the movement of life-giving arousal energy activated by and drawn toward a particular direction (a person, a thing, an activity). Diligently discovering what activates this inner aliveness taps your human potential for resilience and your ability to overcome life challenges by layering experience with emotional richness and personal meaningfulness. Body changes and difficulties can feel like you are losing parts of yourself, and the only option is to grieve and move on. Bodyful practices that you include in your daily life give you the vehicle to engage with your challenges in a way that adds *more* fullness to your experience of your body. This is what we will explore in Section 3, the rhythms of intimacy.

SECTION 3

The Rhythms of Intimacy

8

SHARED VALUES IN ACTION

If you were to enter my office today, hoping to embark on a journey to improve your intimacy, I would encourage you to refine your hopes into actionable intentions—intentions that become daily practices which are specific and relevant to who you are and what is important to you. These are intentions you can fully embody because they *are* you. They offer a shared foundation for you to lean on as you explore how to sync up in somatic flow with each other.

A shared foundation of intention in the form of shared values allows your body to feel safe enough to be close to your partner, to invest your precious energy in growing your connection, and to allow your bodies to relax in each other's presence. This invites you to be more receptive to connection and, of course, pleasure.

These shared values invite you to clarify the sweeping generalizations with which many people enter their intimate relationships. If you are monogamous, what does monogamy mean to you? How does it inform the ways that you interact with each other, and how do you represent your particular brand of monogamy out in the world? If you are non-monogamous, what does non-monogamy mean to you, and how do you infuse non-monogamy values into your daily life? Instead of taking these important relationship structure terms for granted or relying on someone else's definition, you get to define them for yourself based on what is meaningful for your relationship sustainability, inspiration, and evolution.

In this chapter, I will ask you to explore the following questions to help frame and paint the canvas of your intimacy:

- Do you and your partner have meaningful agreements and shared values that support your individual sexuality as well as your sexual relationship with each other?

DOI: 10.4324/9781003508984-12

- Do you feel like you have a sense of purpose when it comes to your sexual intimacy? What are you exploring, working toward, investing in?
- If you are monogamous, what are your monogamy-based values? What have you absorbed from your culture that aligns with your partnership, and what does not align?
- If you are non-monogamous, what are your non-monogamy-based values? This is a relationship structure that is just beginning to find a general social blueprint. As a result, you have been more actively exposed to monogamy values. Notice what monogamy values integrate well into your practice of non-monogamy and which are hindering your relationship?

These are big questions. They begin to peel back the layers to reveal the places where your foundation is strong and flexible and where it is unsteady and unaligned. If you are experiencing relationship challenges, the day-to-day rhythm that you enact is keeping you going, often to the beat of responsibilities and logistics, but not necessarily connected intimately. Perhaps the rhythm is ill-fitting, like a dress or a coat tailored for someone else. Relationships are often entered through a framework that is made for us by the patterns and beliefs of family, culture, or religion. Our intelligent nervous systems organize in a way that helps us conform to this framework and expectations while addressing our individual needs and desires as best we can. We develop coping mechanisms or adaptive strategies that help us get by, but don't necessarily represent who we actually are or what we are specifically striving for. They don't necessarily allow us to express our best and brightest parts!

This is where we can apply the practices of embodied intimacy to your relationship in a way that truly represents and enhances the uniqueness of your dynamic.

Defining and embodying your unique dynamic is a culmination of practicing many of the things we've already covered: Practicing embodied consent and embodied communication, learning your expression of the whole-person sexual response cycle, and practicing a securely attached relationship with your arousal anatomy. All of these practices can now be given roots by (1) defining what is meaningful and supports your unique rhythm, where you both agree to direct your energy, and (2) learning the body connectivity principles and practices that help you live out these values through your body-to-body connection and through the activities and intentions that you prioritize. This is the framing for a genuine and vibrant *shared intimacy.*

Shared intimacy values give you a foundation to set the rhythm in happy times and a place to return to in challenging times when you feel you have lost your way. This is the *why*—why work on your intimate connection? Why navigate the discomfort that arises in the moment? Why work toward the paradigm shift that reshapes how you see the world of your sexuality? *Because this is worthy work.* But what makes it worthy is defined by you. It frames your mutual sense of purpose, creating a container that helps you find common ground even when you have different desire styles or interests, or when you have a powerful emotion in the moment that places the reptile brain (your instinctual hind brain) in the driver's seat, making rash statements and decisions out of fear or hurt feelings. Established shared intimacy values are the stabilizing force and steadfast rudder that steers you through the emotional storm.

Then comes the *how.* How do you make your shared values three-dimensional? How do your bodies connect in a way that *feels like you fit?* This is an inside-out, bottom-up kind of job. Making an agreement is important, but how you actualize it moment-to-moment through your somatic relating is the real work of bringing your values to life. How do you find safety and excitement in your body-to-body connection? How do you navigate differences in pace and rhythm? And how do you align your shared values with your expression of sexual intimacy?

Together, shared values and how you embody them give an inspirational sense of purpose, making a meaningful journey out of the relational work that you are dedicated to.

Let's begin with the *why* and move into the *how.*

The Why—Defining Your Shared Values

We all need something to orient ourselves to, to organize around, and to stabilize our focus, so that we can invest our energy in ways that nourish us and those we love and help us find shared meaning. Like a tree anchoring its roots in the ground in community with other healthy trees and flora, we benefit from something to guide how we navigate and grow. A tree in a community of trees grows its leaves and branches to make space for the other trees around it so that they can all get enough nourishment from light to thrive. In secure attachment, humans do this too. This gives us a sense of *belonging*, that sense that *we are in this together.*

For humans, we find this in how we embody our values. We invest in what we value, and this is what can stabilize you when your moment-to-moment emotions fluctuate. A moment of frustration or hurt feelings does not cause you to quit the relationship when you are stabilized by an underlying agreement that you will work through conflict together in a way that honors your communication styles and validates your emotions—especially when you have a history and body memories of successfully working through moments just like this.

In an intimate relationship, you have values that you share, giving you a sense of the "we." You also have values that you hold individually but don't share, or you have values that are at different places on the priority list. Perhaps you both value traveling, but one of you values relaxation time, a reprieve from your busy schedule, while the other values having adventures. If you have a shared value of supporting each other's nervous systems, you are more likely to schedule in and actively engage with both relaxation and adventure time instead of begrudgingly participating in the other's activity or expressing resentment. Your shared values can support your differences.

You can also have competing values that are not easily supported by a shared value. Perhaps you have kids, and you both want to do your separate activities at the same time, but you don't have trusted childcare. Frustrating, but pretty normal. Again, finding a shared value along with a broader view of the defining features of the life stage that you are in can bring you back to that stabilizing sense of "we." Perhaps you take turns doing your activities and then, when you come back together, practice the intentional transition to check in, share your experience, and celebrate each other's adventures as you remind each other that this is a season of life.

There is also a shadow side to values. One of the shadows of kindness and respect, for example, could mean that you withhold frustrations or hide difficult topics from your partner because you don't want to hurt their feelings or disrupt the harmony of the home. This, of course, doesn't work in the long term and actually causes frustrations to come out sideways as anger or passive aggressive comments, while hiding things breeds mistrust, even when your intention is to protect and maintain harmony.

The shadow side of values shows that there is incongruence between your cognitive understanding and how you are somatically organized and expressing. Our nervous systems are smart—as intimate partners, the body can sense when one of you is being incongruent, and this can feel unsettling. You can sense that your partner is frustrated (whether with you or something else), but they are saying that they are "fine." Creating a shared value of transparency, for example, guides you to share with your partner that, yes, you are feeling frustrated and also are trying to transition into connective time and perhaps just need a bit more space and grace to release the frustration. Your partner gets to say, "thank you for telling me! Since we both value supporting our nervous systems, let me know if I can support you in doing something that helps work through your frustration." This is what begins to build that rhythm of trust when a shared value is enacted in real-time. You can create an environment where you and your partner do not have to silo off your emotions to keep them safe from being invalidated—instead, a shared value of transparency supported by skills to work with your nervous system creates an abundant space to acknowledge and validate hard feelings and work toward reconnection.

The values that my clients quickly name are terms that represent a vast realm of possible interpretations, such as monogamy/non-monogamy, pleasure, eroticism, quality time, touch, or respect. After all, many of these words have been defined by the social institutions that you were raised in. An embodied intimacy practice invites you to take these umbrella terms and personalize them, open them up into their component parts to gather a collection of values that are inspiring and stabilizing to your relationship.

So, when you begin to explore with your partner what they value, it is easy to get caught up in semantics. For example, you and your partner could be practicing the value of quality time by having a relaxing, pleasurable experience together in a hot bath, and one of you will identify this as a form of eroticism—the tension and release that comes with entering hot water and then adapting to the heat and relaxing—while the other one says that the bath was meaningful quality time because it aligns with their shared value of relaxing together—"It's intense and then I relax. So it's not erotic, it just feels good." Rather than get caught in semantics and general terms that people use (like attractive, erotic, or how sex or pleasure is defined), get descriptive with each other using the embodied communication principles. It's okay that you define *erotic* differently—it's your felt experience that matters—the overlap of what feels good to you and the intention. A value that you can articulate intellectually has somatic architecture to it, influencing how you experience (felt sense) and respond (express, interact) in everyday situations.

Here are some journal questions to consider together to discover and get descriptive about your shared values:

1. What is important to you about your intimacy? Cultivating safety? Prioritizing no-pressure time together? Creating space for skin-to-skin contact? Connection and practicing receiving? Emotional connection and playfulness? Make a list of three to five descriptive words.
2. Is orgasm important to you? If orgasm is challenging for one or both of you, what other peak experiences during intimacy are important to you? Peak pleasure moments or peak emotional connection?
3. What is important to you about sexuality? Supporting expression? Getting more comfortable using a meaningful language? Bringing levity to life? Deconstructing from a shaming culture? Permission for consensual pleasure? Exploring some aspect of your sexual identity?
4. What helps you to feel safe enough and present for intimacy with your partner?
5. What is important about intimacy at your current age and life stage?

Identify Shared Values and Complimentary Values

Once you journal with these questions, you may find that you have both similarities and differences. Combine your similarities as *shared values*. Then, make sure you look more closely at the differences—they may actually compliment or support each other. For example, one of you may feel uncomfortable talking about sex in general, and one of you can talk about sex more broadly but may feel uncomfortable expressing personal desires, so two shared values could be (1) creating a safe-enough environment to practice using more descriptive, meaningful language with (2) no pressure to act on the language in that moment. Write these down as your *complimentary values.* Remember to thank your partner for sharing their journaling with you.

Notice what happens in your body as you journal and talk about the above questions. Identifying the somatic experience and architecture of your values helps you to better understand them in yourself, better articulate them in a way your partner can understand, and help you identify when a value expression is present. Can you identify moments where you felt excitement bubbling up through your abdomen, relaxation and softening in your muscles, or an inner interest to lean toward your partner? You may have also noticed moments of feeling more bound flow of body armor in your muscles, posture, and breath activating as you journaled about what is important to you or while you shared with your partner. You know you have arrived at a shared or complimentary value when your body armor softens, and you feel more of that inner stability within yourself with an inner lean toward your partner. If your body feels strongly about it, it is something that matters and would benefit from being communicated in order to feel seen and find common ground.

Let's turn now to the *how*, bringing with you your somatic experience to explore how you can find flow in your body-to-body connection.

9

FINDING SOMATIC ATTUNEMENT

It is an everyday art for two (or more) bodies to come together in somatic or embodied attunement. This is why countless patrons have shown up for millennia to witness the choreography of bodies moving together. Whether a ceremonial dance, ballet or modern dance performance, Cirque du Soleil, or contact improvisation, our nervous systems love the experience of witnessing the flow and grace that is possible when bodies move together. The act of witnessing makes it possible for us to feel within ourselves that experience of flow and grace while also giving us access to a broader repertoire of movement. Through our inner embodied simulation mechanism, witnessing attunement activates an emergent response of inner micromovements or more outwardly expressive movements.

Embodied attunement is an experience that many people long for and actively seek out. Before a wedding, couples often hire a dance instructor—someone to teach them to move in synchrony with each other, as leader and follower learn to listen with their bodies to each other's cues. That first dance after the ceremony is a rite of passage—a moving somatic sculpture of the couple's compatibility. The message of this dance represents to both the witnesses (family and friends) and to the couple themselves whether they are a good fit—does their body-to-body connection feel good? Do they feel desired, respected, honored, and seen by the other? If someone steps on a toe, are they able to transition from a moment of chaos back into flow? Do they recover with humor and grace? This movement dynamic—the moving sculpture of their individual movements coming together to form a third, combined movement dynamic—can continue into the intimate realm of their relationship.

This is the *how* of embodying your shared values.

DOI: 10.4324/9781003508984-13

Embodied or somatic attunement, combined with intentional misattunement, is the fundamental component of secure attachment and bonding whereby your body can *listen* to the body of another on a visceral, feeling level and respond non-verbally in a complementary way—a felt-sense of inner stability with dynamic flexibility to incorporate the felt-sense experience of another. This is the body's ability to say *I see you, I hear you, and I feel you*, as the awareness of your body oscillates between what is being expressed by your partner and what your own body is feeling in response. It is embodied attunement that makes emotional intelligence possible as the non-verbal underpinning of understanding one another, allowing you to participate in each other's emotional life and create a shared experience.

Embodied attunement is something that we all have access to naturally. It can also be refined as a relational skill to improve your relationships, both personal and professional. You can refine this skill by (1) increasing your awareness of your own somatic architecture and (2) increasing your awareness of movement qualities in emotional, boundary, and desire expression.

We all have movement qualities that make us who we are. These movement qualities—the external expression of internal somatic and neural architecture—allow expression of what is felt inside so that we can understand each other, and, when we resonate with an expression, experience somatic and intimate attunement. More than familiarity, this gives us access to the enjoyable feeling of vibing with an intimate partner in a way that makes us feel more ourselves, more alive. It also gives us access to non-verbally responding when our partner is upset—when their nervous system is dysregulated, and they would benefit from accurate mirroring and supportive movement cues in response—which makes it more likely that you will shift into a more regulated and attuned state together. We are, in fact, neurobiologically wired to be motivated to share in the mutual delight of expressive movement with another—this is the bread and butter of social engagement.

You have probably experienced embodied or somatic attunement with your intimate partner. Even though you have moments of feeling awkward or mismatched with each other, you also have the ability to find flow through embodied attunement.

According to Italian neuroscientist Vittorio Gallese, "the shareability of the phenomenal content of the intentional relations of others, by means of the shared neural underpinnings, produces intentional attunement" (Gallese, 2004). The *neural underpinning* that he's referring to is the sensory-motor system of the brain and nervous system. This system allows you to observe others, and, through the mirror neurons found in the sensory-motor system, develop what Gallese calls an internal *embodied simulation*, or "an automatic, unconscious, and pre-reflexive functional mechanism, whose function is the modeling of objects, agents, and events" (Gallese, 2004). These mirror neurons don't just observe others, they create an internal representation and felt experience of another person's embodied expression. As you feel within you the expression of your partner, you can allow movement expression to flow from your own body in response. This embodied response comes from feeling the impact of your partner's expression, like receiving the sound impact from a percussion instrument—we move in response internally as well as through external expression through a change in breath quality, posture, facial muscles, and movement of the musculoskeletal system.

For example, perhaps you've been on a trip, and you are seeing your partner for the first time in a while. As you step inside the door, setting your bags down and saying hello, you look up and your partner is standing near you with their arms open, their face wide with a smile and eyes soft. Your brain creates an embodied simulation of your partner with their open and inviting posture, creating an inner sensation of openness, warmth, maybe even vibrating excitement. This somatic experience culminates in an inner lean toward your partner as you follow the movement impulse to approach them and be held by them.

When seeking out connection, your brain and body work together to seek enjoyment and shared meaning with other people, especially with intimate others, by unconsciously observing their expression, *feeling it in your own body,* and offering a response. From there, your body determines whether the other person's rhythms, pace, use of space, body posture, and overall expression feel familiar to you and whether it feels *good* to your body. This is the somatic foundation of building familiarity and empathy with the important people in your life. Otherwise, why be social at all, if it didn't feel good to us?

This also happens in defensive situations, where you detect ill intent, rejection, or flat affect (no facial expression) from the other person through the embodied simulation mechanism created in your sensory-motor system. This can feel dysregulating to your nervous system, and your body begins to activate body armor. Your partner furrows their brow and raises the tone of their voice, you internally retract, and the muscles around your heart constrict. This kind of mis-attunement with a partner can be uncomfortable and even painful.

Mis-attunement can also create a complementary, inspirational response. For example, if you are feeling nervous during intimacy due to a body change after surgery, your partner might actually feel a sense of confidence that you can move slowly together, communicate well, and find your way into intimacy. Your partner's non-verbal communication is something like, "It makes sense that you are nervous and I trust in our ability to do this together." Your partner's confidence, mis-attuned with but not insensitive to your nervousness, could inspire your nervous system to relax enough to accelerate into arousal and into attunement with each other.

Here are two questions to consider before we continue:

- Are you able to feel in the flow with your partner while also keeping an awareness of yourself and what your body is feeling and wanting?

- When is your body organized in a way that allows you to rest into inner stability with the possibility for new learning and expansion in your intimate relationship? In what context is this true?

Understanding how to find embodied or somatic attunement or intentional mis-attunement is an important skill to heal relational ruptures, find reconnection, and enjoy a sense of flow with each other. Let's look at how you can actively engage with your body's natural ability of embodied simulation to feel each other and connect. We'll then explore the practice of total body connectivity to amplify your ability to express in a genuine and authentic way.

A Practice of Embodied Attunement

It is possible to refine your ability to find somatic attunement and flow with each other through practice—you are literally wired for it! Fundamentally, this learning is about building a bridge between your efficiency/responsibility-focused self and your present-moment, intimacy-focused self. The responsibility-focused you is active when you are in a nervous system state that supports tracking your environment for problem-solving, tracking logistics (that ongoing list or calendar in your head), fairness (who initiates bids for connection more in the way you recognize), historical examples when your partner did or did not meet your need, and so on. Meanwhile, your intimacy-focused self is active when you are oscillating between your own inner desires and the desires of your partner embedded within and referencing the present moment for emotional expression and for enjoyment of relaxed and excited connection. Intimacy-focused awareness engages the instrument of your body—all of your senses, not just seeing and hearing—in a 3D experience that supports your learning/sensing style. The self-reflection that you can access here, combined with embodied communication, supports expressing yourself to your partner congruently, making space for you to be more of who you are.

You are also learning to build a somatic bridge between a defensive nervous system state (SIS) and a receptive nervous system state (SES). Developing a shared embodiment practice to explore how to bridge into connection—a practice where you can learn about how your bodies relate non-verbally through movement, touch, and breath—allows you to be able to access body-to-body flow in a way that feels true to both of you by optimizing the beautiful mechanism of your sensory-motor system. Not moving at either of your individual paces but, instead, *moving at the pace of connection*, where you both are in a reciprocal dance of expression and receptivity.

Moving at the pace of connection in intimacy can be challenging. There are a few things that get in the way of this pleasurable flow experience. Embodiment and expression are impacted by context (environment and human interactions), socialization (how we are influenced to inhabit the body and take up space based on our culture, age, gender, social position, etc.), and by the values and judgments we have internalized about how a "good" partner should show up. This activates coping mechanisms that organize our bodies into protective reactions toward the environment, and away from genuine movement expression.

The first challenge is when people approach their partners only from their own desire and interest—they are moving with their own rhythm and at their own pace, fully self-referencing and not tracking their impact. When I see people approach and interact with their partner only from a self-referenced or self-focused place—without that pause between impulse and action to check in with their partner, like in the embodied consent practice—I often witness the partner retract or shrink within themselves, or they quickly reorganize their body and expression to meet the self-focused partner, a chameleon keeping harmony in the relationship. Neither of these responses indicates that they have felt invited into intimate attunement and are instead in reaction to their partner's approach. It is difficult to intimately attune with a partner who is not in the present moment with you but in the present moment with themselves or in an unconscious reaction place (autopilot).

It makes sense that many people approach sexual intimacy from a self-focused or unconscious place. We are often exposed to sexual behavior from a solo place and are not taught to be relational in arousal. From learning about reproductive-based sex in an awkward and tense environment, to the general silence and secrecy around any earnest conversation about sex, to the consumption of porn and erotic entertainment for personal pleasure, many people develop a self-focused way of approaching sex—they literally have had limited experience in how to navigate sexual contact with more than their own body and they just don't know what they don't know.

Second, I see people approach their partner based on their perception of how they think their partner wants to be approached. This is also a one-sided approach to intimacy, but more disembodied and cognitive. Approaching from your perceived idea of what your partner wants indicates a lack of oscillating present-moment awareness between self and partner, and a lack of understanding of where you are approaching from within yourself. When your body organizes around a more cognitive or strategic state, it often requires you to suppress your own genuine, intimate expression and prevents you from seeing your partner as they actually are in that moment. You can lose track of yourself, causing your breath to be more constricted in the upper chest, your movements to be more rigid and furtive (we call this *bound flow* in the muscular system), giving your partner a sense of anxiousness or hesitance. This can feel unsettling and give your partner a sense of your own incongruence (your own embodied desire and the way you are approaching do not align, or your motivation to approach is unclear). Potential and possibility are lost in a sea of assumptions.

Additionally, because your focus is primarily on your partner, this can often induce in them a feeling of being under a microscope. You have probably organized your body into this more strategic state because you are, actually, considering your partner—perhaps they have a trauma history, or there is a relational wound between you that you are trying to heal, or your partner has a body challenge that they are navigating—and you are trying to match your method of approach to what you think your partner needs to get the best result. You are curating your embodied presentation. Even though this is probably not your intention, being the sole focus of an intimate exchange causes most people in this position to feel squirmy and pressured. This leads me to the next obstacle to embodied attunement.

I also see people either rushing and pushing through to reach a quicker, more spontaneous pace of affection and/or arousal or rushing to align with the arousal of the partner who has a more clear framing to their desire. In this case, I witness a stressed body organization, and I hear things like, "I feel like I should be able to get my body to respond more quickly," or they begin to avoid intimate contact, including affection, altogether because the internal pressure to perform becomes too stressful. When the partner who has a lower desire or who is unclear about what they desire feels pressure to speed up to the higher desire or more clear partner's pace, their nervous system will activate body armor defenses. The nervous system cannot be rushed—it must be invited. So, if the lower/unclear desire partner begins to feel their body armor activating—that is, tight muscles, pulling into the core of the body, anxiousness, and discomfort—they must address this first by meeting the body armor in intensity on a sensory and movement level so they get to the organic release on the other side. It is from this organic release that deep arousal and eroticism emerge.

For example, if you are feeling anxiousness and discomfort, invite you and your partner to slow down to explore an erotic gateway that meets the intensity of the anxiousness. If the anxiousness feels fast and disorganized, perhaps invite your partner to go for a fast walk with you around the neighborhood. This meets the intensity of the pace with a more organized and rhythmic movement to contain the discomfort. As you walk through your local park, focus on a full breath in and a full breath out as your muscles begin to warm; the contra-lateral rhythm of walking begins to soften the feeling of discomfort, bringing dynamic order back to your internal somatic landscape, opening your chest, and opening the frame of your body. As you return home, get a glass of water, and sit together, notice, do you feel the same or different? Can you sit and lean into your partner, shoulder-to-shoulder, and allow a yield to settle you into connection?

Overall, I find that people do not take time to center themselves before transitioning into an intimate connection. Those mirror neurons in your sensory-motor system are smart, and they can tell, through *embodied simulation*, that one or both of you are not centered and in an incongruent state in your expression and, therefore, not available for embodied intimate attunement. I get it. After a busy day with work, responsibilities, or parenting, centering the self and finding attunement can feel like more work. You may expect that if you want intimacy, your body should just shift into a sexual state—and if you don't, you are just too tired for intimacy, any kind of intimacy.

This is where finding what dance/movement therapist Irmgard Bartenieff called *a lively interplay between internal connectivity and external expressivity* can support you to find intimate attunement by identifying the amplitude and volume that aligns with your energy level and interest.

By applying an embodiment practice such as the intentional transition, you can center yourselves then find that interplay between internal connection and external expression to allow your non-verbal affinity to be more genuine, moving from the inside out. This creates an optimal environment to practice attunement.

Let's look at the basic skills for embodied attunement.

Core Skills to Support Embodied Attunement

As you and your partner embark on crafting an intimate attunement practice together, there are a few core skills to incorporate.

Witness instead of watch. Before we talk about what qualities of movement expression to notice, we must talk about *how* you notice. Movement expression can be quite a vulnerable thing! Remember that you both are learning something new about yourselves and how your bodies bridge into connection. This is initially a pre-effort state that you are saying yes to—your body will not be fully coordinated as you activate your learning mind, and you may feel a bit awkward or silly at times. As you witness yourself and your partner through this attunement practice, witness with compassion, non-judgment, and curiosity. Your attention becomes an embrace of kindness and interest as you witness yourself and your partner. Witnessing is a vulnerable practice that, over time, builds a deeper sense of trust in each other when you offer and receive compassionate witnessing.

When you and your partner are connecting—whether sharing your day, practicing the movement explorations found later in this chapter, or attuning to each other for intimacy—you can shift into a *witnessing* quality of focus by widening your somatic landscape with breath and relaxing your body while your partner shares their experience, their desires, and their emotions. As your partner speaks and moves their expression non-verbally, notice the qualities of their movement, tone, and pace. Instead of thinking about how you are going to respond, oscillate your attention inward and notice what happens in your own body as you witness them, and let your partner know what you feel in response. Then share what you see in them, using descriptive words of embodied communication (not labels or assumptions), and ask if you got that right or if your language resonates with them. If your language doesn't feel true to your partner, that's okay! Ask them to tell you more about what language and movement qualities fit their experience. If your partner is witnessing you, thank them for seeing you. And if you are witnessing your partner, thank them for sharing themselves with you. Getting things "right" is not important. A willingness to share, listen, learn, and share gratitude is important. It is the *intimacy* of the moment that matters. Remember that witnessing is a skill that we refine over time.

Oscillate attention between narrow/focused attention and panoramic/expansive attention. Oscillating your attention between focused and expansive attention helps you not to get stuck in habits that are ineffective or create disconnection with the present moment (Winston, 2019). These two types of attention, focused and panoramic, are practiced in meditation and are also supportive when attuning with yourself and a partner.

With narrow or *focused attention*, your awareness is engaged with a specific aspect of yourself or your partner. For example, you may notice tension that forms in your shoulders, a bound flow in your muscles that creates rigidity, as you begin to walk toward your partner to connect, and you may notice some corresponding thoughts (*Do I look silly? Will my partner receive me?*). Or your attention may focus on how lovely your partner's eyes look as you approach them and, as your pace quickens, you notice an excited bubbling in your solar plexus. These examples reveal both the light and shadow of focused attention—the specific attention can amplify fixation on stress, or it can ignite curiosity and excitement in the finer details. Either way, I encourage you to appreciate what you notice and then gently dislodge your awareness from the focused attention and widen your awareness into the panoramic.

Panoramic or *expansive attention* broadens your awareness to take in everything at once. Breathe into your back body, allow your vision to expand into your periphery at the edges of your sight, and allow your attention to engage all your sensations or movement qualities at once, revealing an overall energy, pattern, or shape. Then take in all of your partner at once with your senses including who you know this person to be and what they mean to you. You are creating the space for all of your own experience and all of your partner to inhabit.

Try oscillating between these two qualities of attention, not necessarily following your breath, but allowing yourself time to find something specific to notice and invite curiosity in the qualities that you notice. Once you feel you have landed in the focused attention, shift your awareness to the panoramic, taking all of something in at once. Notice the pace of the transition between inner focus and outer focus with the focused and panoramic attention qualities. Do you notice that you get stuck in a focused or panoramic quality and it's hard to dislodge your attention? Do you shift abruptly into one or the other? Remember, no judgment—you are increasing awareness of your attention habits and working toward practicing both.

Oscillating awareness is engaging with attention as a contemplative practice. Knowing that your embodied simulation mechanism creates a felt experience within you and influences your response, inviting your awareness to embrace the present moment and witness your partner in a holistic way, allows you to respond to more accurate and useful details. Having an easeful and flexible attention helps you embrace the present moment and also supports a balanced nervous system and more easeful and flexible movement and expression.

Expand your senses. As you practice attunement with each other, begin with your eyes closed or your gaze soft on the floor so that you can reach your other senses out to feel your partner in space. The eyes are powerful sensors that can open us up to fixation, interpretation, and assumption if we rely on them first, so give yourself time to *feel the presence of your partner near you* without physical contact or eye contact first.

Sensing with your whole body activates your non-verbal, somatic intelligence so that you can *feel* your way into connection. When you are near your partner, but not touching, the nervous system of your body can see and feel the nervous system of your partner's body. Via your exteroceptive senses—sensory nerve cells designed to sense your environment—the awareness of your body can "see" your partner and pick up cues as to how they are feeling, what their body rhythms are, and what mode their nervous system is in, defensive or receptive.

Slow your awareness and tune into their breath, their pulse, and the rhythm of their presence. Notice your internal impulse toward your partner as you tune in. Put a pause between impulse and action to share with your partner what you notice: What do you notice happens in your body as you expand your senses to feel your partner in space near you? Do you feel an inner lean or pull to get closer or farther away? Do you notice a softening in your body or a mobilizing feeling in your body in anticipation of connection? Speaking descriptively from your experience, let your partner know what you notice.

Tuning into your body-to-body proximity with your partner at this level supports non-verbal attunement and affinity. You can return to this level of sensing when you get distracted or dysregulated during intimacy. Resource early, resource often.

Mirroring, not imitating. Mirroring happens naturally. When we feel safe enough while witnessing someone, our sensory-motor system activates, and mirror neurons start firing, formulating that embodied simulation of the person's experience. This can initiate automatic movement in response that can mirror the quality of movement you are witnessing. Your partner laughs, and you laugh with them. Your partner sways, and you find yourself swaying with them. Mirroring a partner's movement can be a sweet and sensual way to connect without touch, to feel a partner's experience, and to help them feel seen and understood. When we don't feel safe enough while witnessing someone, we may instead activate body armor in response, mis-attuning with them in a protective posture. If you find yourself mis-attuning (your partner laughs and you find yourself pulling into your midline or shifting away from them), ask yourself what your body is telling you and what you may need to reconnect. You may need clarification about your partner's desires, or you may feel uncomfortable with their movement quality. We all have movement preferences and biases, and this is an opportunity to explore different movement qualities with a partner.

Mirroring can feel quite vulnerable for both the mover and the mirroring partner. As you explore your attunement practice with your partner, it is important when you notice you are mirroring a movement to not *imitate* a partner's movement—it's not about matching them or getting it right. Practice the skills of oscillating attention and expanding your senses to allow your mirroring to move from the inside out, acting from your internal feeling of your partner's movement instead of just mimicking how it looks.

As you witness and mirror your partner, say, "As I witness you in this moment, I notice x, y, z sensations/movement qualities in my body." Allow your body to express the movement qualities (we will explore movement qualities later in this chapter) that you experience. They can guide the movement with their own or witness your response movement. Notice which way supports a sense of connection and attunement by exploring how it feels for your partner to receive your witnessing of them. You are sharing impact here, which means that your movement may align with what your partner is expressing outwardly, and it may not. The essence is where attunement is found.

Find your movement dynamic together. I encourage you to not rush the process and take the time to find your movement dynamic together. There is a false idea that has been perpetuated over the generations that not paying too much attention and "letting things happen naturally"—which really just means follow the lead of the higher desire/more clear desire partner—will lead to a good sexual connection. It is true that it is not beneficial to over-intellectualize or overthink connection. It is also not beneficial to trample on the nuance of expression during the on-ramp to arousal to just *get to the good parts*. What if slowing your awareness to the pace of your connection *is* the good part and also the beginning of something good?

The good part is actually slowing your awareness to notice and savor the moments of pleasurable attunement as they arise, the moments where your individual movement qualities begin to combine to create a third, entrained, movement dynamic. This entrained movement dynamic is compelling, creating a centrifugal force around your points of connection that take on the quality of flow.

In the next section, I will share the aspects of movement that you can explore together to enhance where you experience attunement, identify where mis-attunement happens, and how to bridge back into connection.

Take your time. Don't rush contact. Savor your genuine connection.

Find Attunement in Your Movement Dynamic With Dimensions of Movement Expression

Many of my clients have already been to couples therapy. They have learned effective skills to communicate better and to find more emotional connection, they have identified their shared values, yet their sexual intimacy hasn't really improved. They understand each other better, they feel safer, but it doesn't translate into *arousal affinity*—that feeling of being in sync where you both feel pleasurable sensations in your bodies, you feel excited by each other's pleasure, and you are feeling an inner lean toward each other at the same time. It turns out that what the body needs for arousal, while often supported by emotional connection, is more akin to what the body needs to feel a sense of aliveness in a balance of autonomy and connection.

As I said in the whole-person sexual response chapter, arousal is an altered state. Learning to be awake to how the body gets to this altered state, how you ride the waves of this altered state, and how you transition out is where you identify what can get in the way of intimate attunement and identify what allows intimate attunement to flow. Present moment awareness of the embodied movement qualities that get you to attunement and happen during the altered state of arousal is the key to unlocking this awareness and optimizing your connection.

Embodied movements are movement dimensions and qualities that organize into what dance movement therapists like myself call *movement profiles.* Adapted here from the Kestenberg Movement Profile and Labanalysis (Amighi et al., 2018), movement profiles are created with a system of observing and studying how we embody our inner states and non-verbally interact with others. We have different movement profiles for different contexts, emotional states, and nervous system states. The amount of space we take up, the pattern of bound or free flow tension in our muscles, the shapes that we make with our bodies in relationship to others (not the shape of the body itself), and the pace and rhythmic quality of our movements during interactions with others and during transitions between moments and events. Getting movements to trend toward intimate attunement with a partner requires inviting aligned (similar) or complementary (different and compatible) movement patterns. Consider for a moment how your body organizes when you and your partner are laughing and playing together versus when you are in conflict with each other. In these two movement profiles, you can probably detect some stark differences between muscle tension, body posture, proximity, facial expressions, and voice tone.

When it comes to finding intimate attunement with your partner, we can explore movement profiles for day-to-day intentional connection, for the on-ramp to arousal through erotic gateways, for the sexual response cycle, and for the period of time when you transition out of arousal. We also have a "loading screen" movement profile, which is the way your body moves when you are thinking, soothing, or zoning out—a landing place that you settle into between deliberate actions. These are all important realms to support your attunement with each other, and you can identify what combination of movement profiles supports attunement and which inhibit it. Each of these movement profiles helps to reveal the inner states and feelings that create the outer expression. As intimate partners, you are already deeply impacted by your partner's non-verbal expression, and I invite you now to take a closer look and to get curious about what your body is expressing through your movement profiles, what you are sensing from your partner's movement profiles, and how to become more congruent in your expression in order to reveal your combined experience.

Let's explore different dimensions of movement profiles to identify where you find your affinity connection with each other and where attunement is inhibited.

Facing/spacing/pacing: Facing, spacing, and pacing describe your overall orientation to each other's bodies in space, and it's a great place to start learning your combined movement profiles. Let's begin with facing. In *facing*, we explore how it feels somatically for you to be squarely facing each other, turned to the side, or turned away from each other. This is a simple yet surprisingly provocative way to explore your non-verbal impact on each other. You can identify your preferences by asking these questions:

- In what context and at what arousal stage do I enjoy squarely facing my partner?
- In what context and at what arousal stage do I enjoy my partner turned to the side or at a ¾ angle (either my partner or myself turned at an angle)?
- In what context and at what arousal stage do I enjoy my partner or myself turned away from facing?
- In what context do any of the above activate your body armor?
- At what point in intimate connection (affection, fun activity, and sexual intimacy) does your *facing* align or compliment each other?

Try facing each other in different ways and allow both your present moment experience and body memories of each other to surface and share what you notice. Facing is often related to eye contact and to *seeing and being seen* by your partner visually. Eye contact and seeing each other is very stimulating to the nervous system (in both exciting and challenging ways, depending on the context), and I notice that when people are not ready for intimate contact, facing them directly can feel overwhelming. For example, if your partner has a very social job (like a teacher, counselor, doctor, sales associate, etc.), they have probably been talking and making eye contact all day, so when they get home, their nervous system will probably be in the SIS and may need little to no eye contact for a period of time in order to replenish their social battery and shift back into the receptive *SES* state. Eye contact can also be a way of emotionally connecting as a gateway to intimacy and attunement, to witness the expression of emotional congruence between what your partner is saying and the emotion expressed by the movement of muscles around their eyes, what clinical psychologist Paul Ekman calls micro-expressions. Once nervous system regulation, emotional connection, arousal, and interest have built, facing more directly can often be stimulating in an exciting way, so I find that it is best to work up to this. I find that *facing* can be modified in a meaningful way when *spacing* is also considered.

Spacing is the proximity of your bodies in space, and it can support you in feeling your bodily autonomy and tracking your own inner sensations and interests. At the beginning or *on-ramp* phase of arousal, less proximity can either give you a better sense of yourself and a sense of safety and relaxation, or it can create a feeling of anxiety for people who benefit from closer contact to understand the emotional state of their partner.

Greater initial proximity can sometimes make noticing your own autonomous somatic experience more challenging, which can be dysregulating if your partner is over-indexing your experience over their own. This can increase the chance for an entangled or enmeshed dynamic that can throw a wet blanket over your desire. Giving each other the space to connect with yourselves first and then working toward greater proximity allows the space to center, to invite, and then find contact. This makes space for differentiation, personal empowerment and interest, and even excitement. Exploring how the closeness of your bodies allows you to both connect with yourself and also with your partner can be paired with *facing* to modulate the intensity that the proximity creates. Explore your *spacing* preferences with these questions and movement guidance:

- In what context do you prefer your partner in close proximity and directly facing you or partially or fully facing away?
- In what context do you prefer your partner to be in less proximity and directly facing you or partially or fully facing away?
- At what point in intimate connection (affection, fun activity, sexual intimacy) does your *spacing* align?

Pacing is about the rate of movement of your bodies as you explore *facing* and *spacing*. A quicker pace can be exciting, or it can be overstimulating, while a slower pace can create safety or a feeling of awkwardness. Notice your experience with the following questions:

- What pace do you prefer in yourself or your partner when in close proximity?
- What pace do you prefer in yourself or your partner when in less proximity?
- In what context do you enjoy a more abrupt or fast pace, and in what context do you prefer a slower pace?
- At what point in intimate connection (affection, fun activity, sexual intimacy) does your *pacing* align or compliment each other?

Rhythm—fighting rhythms, indulging rhythms: Movement rhythms are created by alternating patterns of tension and release, *bound flow* and *free flow*, in the somatic (muscles and soft tissues) nervous system of the body. When the body has more *bound flow*, the sympathetic (fight/flight/excitement) nervous system is more active and more *fighting rhythms* are expressed. *Fighting rhythms* are not about fighting per se—they are rhythms that are more punctuated and high energy, like when you are jumping rope or biting into crunchy tortilla chips. They require more bound-flow in your muscles and invite more in-breath. When the body has more *free flow* muscle tension, the parasympathetic (rest and digest) nervous system is more active and more indulging rhythms are expressed. Indulging rhythms are more soothing, languid, savoring rhythms, like swaying to lyrical music. Indulging rhythms invite more free-flow muscle tension and more focus on the out-breath.

These two rhythm qualities combined create the flexibility and variability of how the body interacts with the daily environment—fighting rhythms get your energy up, get you where you need to go, they create boundaries and push your growing edges, while indulging rhythms sooth you and invite you to settle in for a moment of nourishment. It is this combination that keeps you alive and regulated, stimulating growth and recuperation.

Whether you have a *spontaneous* desire style or more of a *responsive* desire style, notice if your erotic gateways begin with activities that invoke more *indulging rhythms* or more *fighting rhythms*. Ask yourself, *what helps your body relax enough to be receptive to pleasure and connection?* Indulging rhythms, like a swaying rhythm, can be more sensual and relaxing, or the twisting rhythm can allow for space to flirt and generate arousal. Meanwhile, erotic gateways that invoke more *fighting rhythms,* such as a strain/release rhythm in vigorous exercise, can build energy through tension and offer a pleasurable, organic release.

Sometimes, people in an intimate relationship align in their erotic gateway interests. Other times, couples can have different preferences here. Initially, this can look like a desire difference that creates a challenge in an intimate dynamic. However, by understanding what rhythm qualities support your arousal and enjoyment to initiate the stages of arousal, it's more about timing and supporting each other to have the space to engage your *home base* rhythms and then transition into connection. Notice how the fighting rhythms have a quality of tension and release, while the indulging rhythms have a quality of release that then builds arousal? By engaging in personal erotic gateways with less proximity between you, you can find a place to meet in the middle. For example, the spontaneous desire person could go for a run or a workout, while the responsive desire person meditates or takes a hot bath, giving time for the spontaneous desire person to meet the desired tension and find the organic release on the other side, and then join the responsive desire person as their arousal has started to build. Here are some questions to consider:

- In what context do you find *fighting rhythms* and more *bound flow* to be enjoyable?
- In what context do you find *indulging rhythms* and more *free flow* to be enjoyable?
- At what point in intimate connection (affection, fun activity, sexual intimacy) do your *fighting rhythms* align or complement each other?
- At what point in intimate connection (affection, fun activity, sexual intimacy) do your *indulging rhythms* align or complement each other?
- In what context do you find you prefer indulging rhythms first or fighting rhythms first? Do you prefer to begin with fighting rhythms (high intensity dancing, or exercising) followed by a flowing into indulging rhythms or the other way around?
- Do you find that your attunement benefits from engaging in a fighting rhythm activity on your own first and then joining with your partner in an indulging rhythm? Or do you find that attunement benefits from engaging in an indulging rhythm on your own before joining your partner in indulging or fighting rhythms?

Quality of Transitions: The quality of movement as you *transition* between moments or between events and contexts reveals the underlying quality of emotion and presence within our rhythms. Slowing your awareness around transitional moments, like coming home from work or heading out for exercise, can support or hinder intimate attunement, especially when you try to connect with your partner if one of you is in a stress-laden transition, while the other is centered and ready for intimacy. Transition styles can be abrupt, gradual, and have a high or low intensity, so making space for both of your styles can honor each other's body autonomy and support the on-ramp to arousal and intimacy. Ask yourself about your transition style:

- Where do you find that you have a fast, bound flow, abrupt transition style? Between what contexts or events?
- Where do you find that you have a slower, more low-intensity transition style? Between what contexts or events?
- In what context do you find that you move at a similar pace during transitions in a way that feels like you are in the flow together?
- Perhaps you prefer beginning intimacy abruptly and then decelerating to slow the pace of contact, or you may prefer beginning slow and accelerating the pace as arousal builds?

Volume: Volume is about how much space you take up—your body itself and your body in space. Volume within your body can increase when you take a full breath, softening and opening your inner somatic landscape, and the volume of your body in space can increase by using more of your *kinesphere* (defined by artist and researcher Rudolf Laban (1966) as the amount of space available within reach of your physical body)—basically, this is your available personal space. You may notice in your intimate partnership that one of you expresses more volume in space than the other, often based on gender, context, sociocultural conditioning, and the level of safety felt in the moment. This volume can be from the distal area of your body, as arms reach out to gesticulate and legs extend.

Volume is also based on your quality of breath. When the body is relaxed, a full in-breath expands the body, volumizing your body in space while creating more internal space for sensation, emotion, and supported movement expression. Meanwhile, the out-breath softens the body, allowing you to get closer to yourself as you turn your attention inward. A relaxed body experiences an even flow quality of expanding and releasing, widening and narrowing, with this full in-breath and out-breath. This is when your body will be receptive to pleasure and connection.

When your body is uncomfortable and not relaxed, volume is diminished with a more constricted in-breath and a shortened or restricted out-breath. Instead of volumizing, you may find yourself feeling contained and ready for action, mounting tension that your inner landscape wants to break through, an inner collapse. This is when your body feels it does not have space to widen or be at ease. Pleasure and connection will be harder to access here.

Notice how the relationship between your breath quality at the midline of the body supports or hinders volumizing the core of your body and extension in the distal area of your body through your limbs.

Discovering what your body needs to be able to volumize in space supports the bridging into a safe-enough connection and accessing pleasure.

Explore these questions with your partner:

- In what context do you feel attunement with your partner when they are taking up more distal space? Or when you take up more distal space?
- In what context do you feel attunement with your partner when they are taking up less space and more contained to their midline? Or when you are more contained?
- When your partner is taking up more volume in space, how does your body organize itself to connect with them non-verbally? Do you take up more or less space? Do you approach directly or face to the side? When is verbal communication helpful?
- What happens to your somatic experience when you take a full breath in, volumizing the core and midline of your body? What happens when you volumize your body with breath while doing something pleasurable such as dancing, eating something delicious, or getting a massage?
- Explore taking turns to increase or decrease the space you take up in your kinesphere. What level of kinesphere-use supports your life energy or sexual energy able to move through your body?

Shaping: *Shaping* is not about the shape of your body—it is descriptive of the way that your body creates shapes as you move through space and while interacting with others. Shaping in space and in relationship can be expressed as a *growing* toward or a *shrinking* away with both sides of your body at the same time (bipolar). It is the emphasis on the movement that gives clarity to the non-verbal message. For example, by hollowing your chest, your shoulders could be curling in as a protective arch around your heart, or you could be reaching toward your partner's hand with your back body. You could also round out your chest, pressing outward from your sternum, as you widen and open your heart for contact, or you could be retracting your back body from contact with something behind you.

Growing and shrinking could also be expressed in a unipolar way, either growing your side body toward your partner to lean into their shoulder or leaning your side body away from them to disconnect shoulders to either see them better or remove connection due to irritation.

Subtle movements of shaping can send a message of wanting to connect or disconnect, of leaning into and responding to pleasurable touch or leaning away from noxious or unwanted touch.

Explore with your partner qualities of shaping toward and shaping away, growing and shrinking your posture to learn about your dynamic.

Explore the following together:

- What do you notice happens in your body when you *grow* your front body toward your partner? Begin one at a time and then try both of you *growing* your front bodies toward each other. What happens? Try adding bound flow to your muscles as you do this, then free flow to your muscles as you explore. Which version supports a sense of intimacy between you?

- What do you notice happens in your body when you *shrink* your front body away from your partner? Begin one at a time and then both of you *shrink* your front bodies away from each other. What happens? Try adding bound flow to your muscles as you do this, then free flow to your muscles as you explore. Which version supports a sense of intimacy between you?
- Position yourselves side by side and try unipolar *growing* and then *shrinking* your side bodies toward and away from each other. Notice how this feels and whether bound flow or free flow in your muscles supports a sense of intimacy.
- Now, what happens when both of you get to *grow* and *shrink* your shaping in space based on your inner, genuine impulse when you are near each other? Do you find that this helps you to titrate your body-to-body relationship in order to balance presence with yourself and connection with your partner?

As you do some reconnaissance with these shaping qualities, share with each other when you felt the most attuned and connected with each other and when you felt yourself and your partner in sync with each other.

10

MOVEMENT FUNDAMENTALS AND ATTACHMENT DYNAMICS

There is a unique movement quality that runs throughout the different movement profiles that you embody in the many contexts of your life—this is your *movement personality* (Słowiński et.al.,2016*)*, the expressive qualities that are the unique ways that you embody yourself in a way that makes you *you.* For example, everyone laughs, but we each have a unique laugh that allows our loved ones to easily pick us out of a crowd. We all have movements that we automatically express for stress relief (like rolling the head and neck or smoothing gestures through our hair), but the way we do it is unique to us. These are the expressions of our somatic architecture and motor patterns with a personalized flair. It is this flavor that we find attractive in our partner—their quirks and essence coming through in the dynamic movement of the human body.

Embodying yourself to the fullest potential of your movement personality allows more of you to connect with your partner. By incorporating movement fundamentals into your bodyful intimacy practices, you can bring this potential to life in your day-to-day. The dynamic components of movement fundamentals developed by Irmgard Bartenieff, a German dancer, choreographer, and physical therapist in the mid-20th century, who believed that the connectedness of the body allowed for a more full range of movement and personal expression. This is an encouragement to "come back to the life of the movement!" as Barenieff would say, to "fill it with yourself . . . otherwise, it is simply an imitation" (Hackney, 2001, 33). Her movement support system guides you to not just do the movements but to *be your movements—your movements are you.* These movement fundamentals offer intimate partners a practical method to enhance and volumize the inner connectedness of the body when engaging in play, affection, and sexual intimacy.

DOI: 10.4324/9781003508984-14

Connecting on this deeper level with your movement embodiment supports unraveling the body armor that has restricted and minimized your movement to serve as a survival strategy, concealing the fullness of your inner erotic map. In a society stuck in an adolescent stage of sexuality, we often carry body narratives that inhibit genuine intimate expression. Instead, as you discover what your body needs to feel safe enough to manifest your inner experience of pleasure and desire as outer movement expression, you begin to rewrite the body narrative of your potential. It gives you the opportunity to pick up the developmental threads that had been dropped due to a lack of holistic sex education and the pervasiveness of sexual shame in order to evolve and mature both your experience of yourself and how you express to your intimate partner.

As you express your facing/spacing/pacing, rhythms, transitions, volumizing, and shaping in space, you can incorporate these movement fundamentals to support filling your movements with yourself—sourcing movement from an inner supported savoring of the pleasure of being in a body. This will help you increase congruence between inner experience and authentic outer expression for deeper intimate attunement with your partner. When you are grounded in your body and expression, more of you is available for relational interplay and ready to receive the nourishment of connection. Bartenieff's *movement fundamentals* that I include here are: *breath support; sequencing from core connectivity or phrasing; dynamic alignment; and spatial intent.* These are the elements that support her first fundamental principle of Total-Body Connectivity, which says that the whole body is connected—a movement in one area of the body affects the whole. The following movement fundamentals use this principle to our advantage to intentionally shift the somatic state into one of genuine expression and receptivity to connection.

Breath Support: "Breath brings life and movement" (Hackney, 41). Movement without breath support feels like a hollow, restrained expression, a performance of affection that conveys little emotion or desire. Holding the breath to the shallow midline of the body restrains feeling and restricts vulnerability—a survival mechanism to protect the self from unwanted touch, from the assumptions of affection, or from the arousal non-concordance of present moment pleasure mixed with discomfort or an unsettling body memory.

With the support of your breath, you invite a wise and mobile foundation to carry your movements while moving with, not against, the available structure of your muscles and bones. Your full in-breath presses into your inner somatic structures, an internal shaping that tells your body where to widen and open to make room for more breath, more sensation, more openness, and expression.

Breath support is the foundation of all life processes and movement expression. When you are unsure how to ground yourself during an intentional transition or are unsure of how to begin connecting with a partner, begin with your breath. Invite a full breath in and notice how your body begins to move of its own accord—move with the movement of your breath as you elongate your spine on the in-breath and shift or shake out any movements on the out-breath. Continue until your inner somatic landscape feels wider and your muscles feel more settled into an easeful in-breath and out-breath rhythm.

I find that tuning into the natural world can help to find breath support. When we connect with nature, our embodied simulation mechanism of the sensory-motor system gives us a felt-sense of the elements—we feel the water flowing in the stream, the wind moving across our skin, or the ocean powerfully ebbing and flowing. Invite your breath to follow the swaying rhythm of wind, or the building and releasing of the ocean swell. Natural forces can be a powerful and clear reminder of your capacity for breath support.

Phrasing—Sequencing from core connectivity: "Kinetic chains of muscular action are set up in the moment of the initiation which sequence and follow-through to complete the phrase" (Hackney, 47). The practice of sequencing movement from the core of the body or from the core of a sensation—a series of micromovements gradually unfolding in order from core to periphery, culminating in a larger movement expression—supports a deep connection to internal desires and motivations and supports a genuine invitation to an intimate partner. Movement that sequences from the origin point of the sensation of desire for connection feels congruent, clear, and courting attunement—an emergent and continuous movement that comes directly from a sensation of pleasure, of longing, of genuine interest. Intentional sequencing prevents performative or imitative movement. Sequencing through the kinetic chains of muscle and bone encourages you to discover the movement as you go—no agenda or expectation. Moving and being moved at the pace of sequencing also gives space for your partner's movement to join yours as you discover together where your combined movement sequencing takes you.

Couples who are struggling to connect often express more hesitant and disjointed or restrained movements toward each other. As a result of the somatic body armor that we develop in response to the disembodied and performative teachings about sexuality, full sequencing of movement is often reduced to disconnected movements that originate from the periphery of the body or movement that is interrupted and doesn't get sequenced from the core to the periphery—in other words, when we feel disconnected from ourselves or our partners, we feel anxious or nervous, movement either feels performative or interrupted and unexpressed altogether.

Incorporating the sequencing of movement from the core of your body or the core of sensation allows you to directly source your movement from your inner feelings toward your partner instead of your movement being sourced from your idea of how you should look or what you think your partner expects.

Furthermore, incorporating breath support with sequencing invites the breath to do what it does—support aliveness! It guides you to shift, slow down, and travel alongside the movement being expressed instead of rushing past awareness of yourself or your partner or pushing past discomfort from painful muscles or joints.

How do you incorporate this into your bodyful practices together? As you stand near your partner, take a few moments to really see them and feel them (without touch) in space. Notice how your internal landscape feels as you see them, discovering within the emergent sensations in response to their presence. You may notice a feeling of excitement or a feeling of relaxed enjoyment in being near them. Breathe around this sensation, supporting it with breath as it gradually amplifies and reveals the deeper characteristics of the sensation. Excitement becomes expanding tingling, like stars in an expanding galaxy, while relaxed enjoyment becomes widening and melting of muscles and bones, increasing the surface area of your body. Notice the directional quality of the sensation as you begin to sequence the movement that is already happening within, inch by inch through the connective muscles and bones, allowing the movement to continue along the path toward your end-points (hands and feet, crown of the head, tailbone). The in-breath supports the sequencing out, while the out-breath supports the yielding at the completion of the movement.

Notice how it feels within your own body to sequence movement toward your partner and how it feels for them to sequence their movement toward you. Does it feel more vulnerable, more clear, or more exciting? Explore with each other while practicing embodied consent.

Dynamic Alignment: "Physiologically, all activities of the body function maximally to the degree that they maintain balance even in motion just as philosophically / psychologically, our lives depend on the same principle" (Hackney, 97). Dynamic alignment is about the head–tail connectivity of the body and the continual three-dimensional adjustments that the body makes while in motion or while standing in stillness. Incorporating dynamic alignment with internal support prepares you for both stability and mobility in your body-to-body connection.

Fluidity in stability-mobility with your head–tail connection and micro-movements in your whole-body connectivity allows for in-the-moment-to-moment adjustments, improvisation, and curiosity as you explore your world and as you interact with your partner. This ability to have both flexibility and stability in your three-dimensional adjustments supports embodied consent as you and your intimate partner navigate the dance of desires and boundaries without becoming rigid in your muscles or losing your balance. For example, with dynamic alignment, you are less likely to lose your bodily or emotional balance when your partner asks you to slow down (perhaps they are uncomfortable or are experiencing arousal non-concordance)—instead, you will gently shift into your back body to make space for curiosity, modulating the pace of your desire without losing track of yourself, slowing your awareness to meet the pace of your partner again. You get to say, "I am here. I am with you," honoring your own desire while considering the state of your partner—stability in mobility. Dynamic alignment in your head–tail connection also supports the balanced acceleration of attuned arousal. Flexibility in the mobility of your spine as your arousal builds together allows for the micro-adjustments of pace and body position to keep your arousal buoyant together. You are less likely to outpace your partner's rhythm or lean too heavily on your arousal accelerator or break, and if you do, you are more likely to seamlessly re-center yourself to attune to the shared rhythm again.

Experience Dynamic Alignment: Stand facing your partner a few feet apart. Visualize a fountain of water beginning at your feet and gently surging upward through your legs, hip joints, joining into one stream just below your ribcage and flowing up your torso along the front of your spine, through your neck, and out through the crown of your head. Allow the stream of water to create inner buoyancy. Notice the orchestra of micromovements that your body makes to keep you around your midline in the vertical world.

Take turns stepping toward each other, noticing the impact of proximity on your dynamic alignment. With embodied consent, you may include touch—connecting the palms of your hands or placing your hand over your partner's heart. Do you find that your body leans slightly toward your partner as they step closer, or do you feel an inner lean away from them? No judgment here if you lean toward or away—the body is accommodating a change in proximity with what it needs to find balance, connecting with the self while in relationship. Allow your body to sequence the lean through your whole spine, the inner stream flowing your musculoskeletal structure toward your partner or away from your partner, then flowing back to your midline. Like a tree swaying in the wind, sequence movement through the body with the support of your breath, making structural micro-adjustments along the way for the lean to be as easeful and fluid as possible. Feel the inner stability in your mobility.

Spatial Intent: "The inner intent of each unique human being influences how his/her body moves and patterns movement. (This inner attitude need not be conscious to be operative.)" (Hackney, 43). Spatial intent describes the directional purposefulness of your inner feelings and desires that organize the body and the movement that is produced. Your outward spatial movements reveal your inner intention for the quality of proximity, or closeness, that your body is hoping for.

A bodyful practice that explores spatial intent invites you to look within when you feel your body reaching for and moving toward your partner. This is where you discover from where within your body your movement originating from, what is the need underneath the movement impulse, what is the emotional quality, where in the space is your body directing you, and how is it getting there (you can move toward or away from a partner in a direct line or in a more indirect, circuitous manner, and with bound or free muscle tension flow, and with different transitional qualities like slow, abrupt, high, or low intensity). It is this somatic information that supports congruence between your intention and your action. The invitation here is to make the intent fully *intentional*, meaning that you are awake and aware of how you are approaching your partner, moving, and being moved by your intention for contact.

Experience spatial intent: Stand across the room from your partner and consider what you enjoy about seeing them. Engage breath support to volumize sensations within your somatic landscape and support the structure of your body to allow these sensations the space to express their inner movement qualities. Notice the sensations that happen in your body as you focus on what you enjoy about them and notice if a movement impulse arises (perhaps, e.g., to move closer to them to hug/be held by them). Describe to your partner what you notice in your own body (when I see you, I notice a warm, opening sensation in my chest, and I notice my movement impulse is to follow that opening sensation to hold you). Invite your partner to share what they feel in response (contact has already happened without touch!) and if they want to invite you to hug them. Try following that feeling, slowly, in a direct line first. Then try following that feeling, slowly, in an indirect line. Encourage your partner to share how each directional quality of spatial intent expression felt and which expression felt most attuned to how they are feeling.

Other Fundamentals to Include in Your Bodyful Intimacy Practice: Notice that all of the fundamentals begin with connecting with yourself first and then connecting with your partner. This is a core part of your bodyful intimacy practice for several reasons. First of all, your partner is going to feel safer expressing themselves if they know that you are tracking yourself—they can trust that if you need or want something different, you will tell them. No mind-reading or guesswork is necessary. This allows both of you to relax into the pleasure and connection of the moment and find yourselves in attunement. Second, if you have a compassionate self-awareness of your somatic expression, you are less likely to get lost in your partner's experience, worrying about their pleasure, and less likely to get stuck in your head and not in your body (the place where enjoyment happens). When you can dislodge your attention from a stuck place and oscillate awareness from you, to your partner, to your connection, then back to you, you will be able to drift into the liminal space of attunement.

Another fundamental movement principle to practice is to breathe into the back body for grounding and deceleration of the momentum of arousal. Arousal is often a forward-moving, momentum-building experience, and this can cause people to outpace their partner in a way that can feel disjointed, even pressuring. By breathing into your back body, your somatic awareness is gently guided to slow your pace and intensity without shutting anything down.

Also, when arousal is accompanied with discomfort or trauma organization in the body, breathing into the back body supports centering, grounding, and initiates regulation of the dorsal-vagal response of the nervous system (the freeze or shutdown response in the perception of a threat) to get you back into your more regulated, easeful, and relational ventral-vagal state. If you know that your dorsal vagal state activates during intimacy with your partner because of a past trauma or relational wound, work together to slow your pace, breathe into your back bodies, and share what could support you to feel safer in the moment.

Explore Your Embodied Intimate Attunement

Consider the following questions to learn about the somatic organization that supports your intimate attunement. Refer to the earlier sections of this chapter and list the movement qualities you notice in yourself and your partner in the following contexts:

1. In what context (environmental, emotional) do you find yourselves in synchrony with each other?
2. In what context do you find yourselves out of synchrony with each other?
3. In what context do you both feel good in your bodies while together?
4. When do you like yourself (how you feel in your body and your personality characteristics that get expressed) in your partner's presence?
5. Based on the movement profiles covered above, what are the movement qualities you are expressing at these times (breath quality, rhythm, pace, sequence of movements, proximity, spatial intent, shaping)?

Once you list the movement qualities for each question, you have a series of movement profiles. Notice when each of your movement profiles comes together in a complementary or synchronistic way. Take a moment to express these movements with each other and appreciate the moments that you are in attunement! Notice how you transitioned into connection that made these moments possible—this is the bridge into intimacy that you will benefit from referencing in the future, as it informs the pathway that your body takes to transition from disconnection into connection.

Support Your Attachment Dynamic With Movement Fundamentals

A secure relationship attachment makes space for feeling safe enough to lean in, to be vulnerable, and to be present without expectations, while also introducing some play and exciting, novel elements to sexual intimacy. In other words, you feel safe enough to take a few risks while being able to receive the pleasure of connection. You feel relaxed and also open to excitement.

Unfortunately, many people have adopted avoidant or anxious attachment patterns in relationship to their body, to their sexuality, and with the sexuality of their partner. As a society, we have an anxious/avoidant attachment with sexuality, so take a moment to see if that feels true for you too. Common ways this can look are: Being sexual only with the lights off, anxiety in anticipation of sex causing quick ejaculation or lack of arousal/orgasm, being unable to verbalize to a partner your interests or a "no" to something that you don't like, discomfort talking about sex, or obliging to sex when you are not in the mood or as a peace-keeper for your relationship. These are all indications of an insecure attachment with the body and sexuality. When insecure attachment is present, whether anxious or avoidant, receiving pleasure or emotional connection is challenging. Like putting water on duck feathers, the potential for pleasure or emotional connection just gets deflected because the body is not organized in an open way to receive; it is organized to defend and protect.

When we practice the rhythm of secure attachment, the body relaxes and is able to trust that nothing will be forced or needs to be avoided. A secure attachment rhythm in sexuality with yourself is a pattern that supports embracing the natural variability of your arousal anatomy and sexual response in a way that allows you to transition in and out of connection easefully with yourself, to experience ownership over your own challenges and discomforts while having compassion for yourself, and using your voice to share your desires and advocate for what you need for your challenges. A secure attachment rhythm in sexuality with an intimate partner is a relational pattern that supports you to connect intimately, and when one partner feels hurt or misunderstood by the other, they can step away, regulate themselves, and connect with the partner again, being welcomed back by their partner, to share their experience and explore as a team what came up and how that interaction could have gone better. When you and your partner have a secure attachment rhythm, even if you have anxious-avoidant undertones (depending on the context, you can have different attachment styles), you can feel challenging emotions and still give each other the space to regulate yourselves, trusting that you will welcome each other back into connection and rely on your teamwork to work it out. There is just enough security to trust the connection and just enough risk to give each other the space to be ever-evolving individuals.

When partners cultivate a rhythm of secure attachment, they are more likely to experience fully embodied pleasure because a balance of security and excitement encourages a more regulated nervous system. A regulated, safe-enough nervous system is more attuned to pleasure and receptivity to connection, while insecure attachment creates dysregulation in the nervous system, creating the conditions for compulsive sexual behavior, low desire, and a general inhibition of satisfying pleasure.

In *Mating in Captivity* (2007), sex therapist Esther Perel highlights a conundrum: love and desire, she says, need different things to thrive. I believe that this is true when love has a quality of enmeshment to it, where you and a partner *fall asleep* in your committed relationship, taking each other for granted, viewing each other (and yourselves) through a veil of assumptions, and not feeling okay if your partner is not feeling okay. To cultivate love with desire, you need to establish a love that values the differentiation of individuality, a bodily autonomy that maintains a structure that supports time invested in each other, as well as time invested in continuing to develop yourselves as individuals. Each attachment dynamic is a rhythm between you and a partner, and it is beneficial to put the content to the side and focus on your body-to-body expression. Let's explore the common attachment style dynamics in relationships and how to use the movement fundamentals to create more balance and liveliness in your connection. Remember that, depending on the context, you can have different attachment dynamics.

Anxious Attachment/Enmeshment: Enmeshment or entanglement is a form of insecure attachment where both partners exhibit an anxious attachment style toward each other. Someone with an anxious attachment style is also referred to as a *wave* (Tatkin, 2012), as they are more often influenced by their environment and the emotional state of those around them. An enmeshment pattern compels you to make decisions based on what you *think* your partner needs, often at the expense of your own—their distress (or perceived distress) overwhelms your system, and you feel like it must be resolved before you can rest. You set aside your feelings and needs to tend to your partner first. You are inclined to not see your partner as capable of handling their own emotional journey, or their distress (or perceived distress) makes it difficult for you to relax and focus on your own experience. You both have the *we just need to resolve this distress quickly so we can feel connected and move on* kind of feeling.

In movement fundamental terms, an enmeshment pattern inhibits dynamic alignment as you lose a sense of your stability, leaning too far into/toward your partner with bound flow. Your breath quality is often higher up in your chest with a rapid pace. You may find that how you shape your body in relationship to your partner is not congruent with how you feel, that is, growing your body toward when you may want to shrink your body away or grow your body toward a more relaxing activity or seek comfort through petting a family cat or dog.

In sexual intimacy, you are often focusing more on your partner's pleasure and have a hard time asking for something different for yourself because you don't want to hurt your partner's feelings. This is accompanied by bound flow in your muscles, hypertonic and unable to relax into the moment, or neutral flow as you find yourself hypotonic and sensation muted.

If you find yourselves in an enmeshment dynamic, try stepping back from each other before intimacy to arrive in your own body through breath support, allowing your breath to shape you from the inside out, exploring how you are feeling in the moment and what your body may need to land more fully in the present moment. This is you finding your autonomous self before connecting with your partner, encouraging you to bring your defined self into a differentiated interconnection—defined individuals coming into connection. Breathe into your back body. As you step closer to each other, practice oscillating your attention between what you feel in your own body and what your embodied simulation detects from your partner. If you notice an assumption arising (my partner doesn't want to explore this with me), breathe into your back body and ask them if you got that right—if your assumption is correct, the other partner can take a moment to explore what they need to be more invested in the moment of exploration. Offer an appreciation and honor their individual emotional journey as a capable human. Continue the practice of oscillating your attention and engaging breath support as you continue your intimacy time with touch and sexual contact.

Anxious-Avoidant Attachment Dynamic: Anxious-avoidant dynamic is a common dynamic in intimate relationships—one partner consistently pursues the other for emotional connection and a sense of togetherness, while the other partner prefers connection with themselves in an independence-first way of operating (Atkinson, 2005) or just generally has a difficult time connecting intimately at all. The avoidant attachment style is often referred to as an *island* (Tatkin, 2012) attachment strategy because they prefer to be insular, more often taking care of themselves emotionally and spending more time emotionally or physically distant than their anxiously attached counterpart. These are people who learned that expressing their emotions in their family of origin wasn't safe or wasn't welcomed—they didn't receive accurate or supportive attunement, so they learned to regulate themselves on their own. These could also people who have trauma organization in their body from prior relationship violations. Islands still want connection, but it is challenging to feel emotionally and/or physically vulnerable. They find that they become overwhelmed quickly by the emotional expression of a partner and must retract to find themselves again.

On a somatic level, those with a primarily avoidant attachment often experience bound flow muscle tension in and around their chest, solar plexus, and shoulders with a more rigid head–tail connection, making their alignment less dynamic and more unyielding.

People with primarily an anxious attachment style, a *wave*, often make the assumption that if the avoidant partner takes time for themselves, they do not want to connect or don't like their partner when actually the avoidant partner just gets overstimulated and needs a low stimulation environment, time with their hobby, or physical movement to settle their nervous system.

The anxious partner has the opportunity to widen their resource pool and refine their ability to regulate themselves as the avoidant partner takes their intentional time with themselves.

Meanwhile, the avoidant partner makes the assumption that the anxious partner is a bottomless well, so they avoid contact instead of asking the partner what they actually need at the moment for fear they will get swept up in hours of contact that they are not prepared for. Sometimes a good hug and acknowledgment are all that the anxious partner wants in order to land into a more secure attachment state.

If you find yourself in an anxious/avoidant dynamic, the anxious partner can use the bodyful skills of the intentional transition to regulate their nervous system enough to connect to their own midline, explore what is underneath the buzzing or shakiness, and identify the movement impulse for connection before they approach the more avoidant partner to request a hug or a few moments of connection—using language such as, "I notice that I'm missing you and want to spend some time connecting." Meanwhile, the more avoidant style partner can engage breath and breath-directed movement to explore what they need to soften their body armor to connect with their more anxious style partner, for example, "I notice I'm feeling the need for movement before I can relax with you, so I'm going to go for a 20-minute run and then check in with you to connect." Knowing how to work *with* your nervous system is the key.

Ambivalent Attachment

Ambivalence is a state where you are experiencing conflicting feelings at the same time. You want closeness but also don't feel emotionally safe enough to lean into your partner, not because they are untrustworthy, but because you have a hard time trusting in general. So, instead of softening into contact, you find yourself pulling back, withholding vulnerable emotions, getting close, and then abruptly retracting. People with ambivalent attachment styles often had parents who were inconsistent in their expression of love and care for whatever reason, and the child learned a rhythm of inconsistency—you lean in, your partner leans in, you tighten and lean away, they lean away, and you lean in again or walk away completely. It can feel confusing to both you and your partner, so slowing down to explore this dynamic on the moment-to-moment level is helpful.

When you are practicing the facing/spacing/pacing exercise from earlier, allow yourself to walk toward or lean toward your partner until you feel the rising tension of body armor. Let yourself pause. Ask yourself, "What is this body armor protecting me from?" Allow yourself to follow the impulse to lean away by walking backward a step or two. You can let your body sway forward and backward as you explore this question. Let your partner know what you discovered and perhaps something that they said or a way that they moved that activated the ambivalent rhythm (not about blame, just gathering information). Ask your partner what happened to them in that moment. Your assumption of what might be underneath their words or movements may be incorrect, an old story that the ambivalence is fueled by. You get to learn that when their muscles tightened for a moment as they shifted feet, they were anticipating that you might retract or they were simply shifting off of a painful foot, instead of your interpretation that they were bracing for contact with you that they didn't want. It is important that you get to pair their movements and words with their intention to support resolving the dilemma of ambivalence. Then ask yourself, "Do I feel more settled? What do I need to feel safe enough to step toward my partner again?" Practice stepping toward and away as you explore the contradictory feelings. When you feel ready, practice moving toward your partner and requesting contact and then stepping away again. Partner, offer gratitudes to your partner, let them know you see them, and honor their body autonomy during this exploration. You want more consistent contact, and so do they; it's just that they have an attachment rhythm to learn to complete and find ground within themselves while remaining open toward you.

If you find yourself in an anxious-avoidant (wave-island) or ambivalent attachment dynamic, you have the opportunity to learn what your body needs to transition into connection (island) and what your body needs to regulate on your own and show up for intimacy feeling more centered (wave). By taking a few moments to check in (see the intentional transition in Chapter 3), both of your attachment styles can be honored. Over time and diligent practice, you will find that you are less anxious, less avoidant, and less ambivalent as you settle into a rhythm of secure attachment more often. While an increase in stressful life conditions can cause an old attachment style to resurface, don't worry! You did not lose all of your progress. You have the skills and relational practices to get back to the secure attachment that you earned.

11

ATTUNEMENT THROUGH CONTACT

Bodyful Touch Practices

Diana and John sit across from each other on my office couch. Both are exhausted. "We didn't sleep well again. The baby woke up at 3 a.m., so I fed him, but he didn't go back to sleep until about 5:30 a.m." Diana's eyes are strained with dark circles beneath, hands are tightly clasped, and muscles are tense from the effort of sitting up. John, her partner of 5 years, sat still next to her, limbs tight to the midline of his body. "I just don't know how to help." "How about we take a break from talking about your challenges today and try something different," I offered. I suggested that we do a bodyful touch practice that they could take with them to adapt at home.

After describing the whole process, my clients agreed, and I encouraged Diana to receive touch first. She clearly had nothing left to give today, and she quickly agreed. As I guided them through the practice, Diana asked to be able to lay on the floor and just have John touch her head. I guided John to connect with himself first, to explore his somatic experience of how he feels about his exhausted beloved. Once his breath deepened, his body visibly widened, and his shoulders softened, I invited him to connect with Diana, beginning with what I call "stillness touch." Stillness touch is where you allow your hands to softly land on your partner's body, letting gravity determine the pressure. Within 30 seconds, Diana began belly-breathing for the first time in session (I had been working with them for two months), her hips softening over the floor as her brow unfurrowed. I encouraged John to gently cradle Diana's head with both hands, holding the weight of her head off the floor. As I invited Diana to breathe into the back of her neck and head where John's hands held her, tears streamed down the sides of her face, and she released an audible out-breath sigh.

Once the bodyful touch practice concluded, they turned to each other and shared their experience. Diana leaned her body slightly toward John and shared

DOI: 10.4324/9781003508984-15

how cared-for she felt. "I felt totally held by you, like you were only present with me, and I could totally let go. I haven't felt that in such a long time!" She seemed almost energized as she shared, brighter and more focused. John said he was so glad he had that opportunity to help her feel that, then he turned to me and said, "I didn't realize it was that simple."

Body-to-body connection is the primal language of intimacy. Without words, touch can communicate an immense amount of information: how you feel about someone, the state of your nervous system, intention, and so much more. Touch can encourage your nervous system to shift into a more relaxed, receptive, and regulated state, as evidenced by the popularity of massage therapy. It can be an offering of love, care, relief, and a meaningful way to give someone access to pleasure. It is a language that speaks the truth about the quality of connection when words are not enough.

Human touch is so powerful that without it, babies' brains and bodies don't develop. Without touch, adults don't thrive and experience higher levels of emotional and physiological dysregulation, alienation, and loneliness, making them more susceptible to disease. Consensual human touch has an immediate physiological and emotional effect, almost instantly soothing the heart or evoking desire.

Whether intentional or not, touch can also hold the energy of taking something for one's own enjoyment, as we discussed in the embodied consent chapter. This is why embodied consent is a critical relationship skill to practice when sharing touch with a partner.

Through safe-enough touch, we learn when to be daring, pressing into the growing edges of our capacity, and we learn when to yield as a movement, a softening and opening, unfurls from within. Like a finger on an acupressure point that sets into motion a whole series of unlocking tension areas in the landscape of muscle, touch can unlock the deepest structures of our brain to encourage development, inner stability, integration of self, and yes, a deeper bond with a beloved.

Neuroscientist Stephen Porges (2011) says that safety in proximity leads to touch, and safety in touch leads to deeper bonding between people. When partners connect physically with each other in pleasurable ways, they are continuing to weave the threads of active interconnectedness into their relationship—through touch, they tell each other that they are a safe place to be. And when this pleasurable touch has the effect of involuntarily moving their bodies closer, volumizing with breath, and leaning into each other's touch, there is a compelling magic that has awoken in them—a body that can soften and move and express is a body that is regulated and safe enough to let themselves be felt. This is the magic at the foundation of genuine passion, a gateway into expanding our potential to experience the fullness of life through the flow of touch between bodies.

However, this kind of expansive flow can feel elusive if touch between intimate partners feels uncomfortable. The body carries its touch history within muscles, tissues, and reflexes into relationship, impacting how we give and receive touch, as well as influencing how touch is coded or interpreted within our hearts and minds and bodies. If someone has experienced safe-enough touch throughout their life, they will approach intimate contact with a partner with openness and interest. However, if someone has experienced human contact in their life that has not felt safe, or experienced social marginalization that caused them to feel unsafe around others, they will need support from a partner to rewire their relationship with human presence and touch. While my client John and Diana felt that the positive impact of touch was so simple, this is not always the case.

During my intake session with Emily and Sarah, it became clear that embodied consent and safe-enough touch would be a primary focus of their work. Both are queer, cis-gendered women, and both experienced feeling physically unsafe in their lives. Sarah says that she had been assaulted by a former partner and now has a complicated relationship with touch. Sarah describes how she and Emily could be sitting on the couch cuddling, totally at ease, and when Emily touches her in a more sensual way, Sarah finds her whole body will tighten, retract, and she'll pick up her phone to start scrolling, dissociating with distraction. Emily says she feels rejected in these moments, like she's done something wrong. "But I'm a safe person!" Emily says, "I would never hurt her." I reflect to them that Sarah's nervous system is protecting her by disconnecting from the uncomfortable feeling, a body memory that surfaced from a quality of touch that felt familiar to a prior, threatening situation. I explained that the need for the body to protect is so strong that it generalizes the sensation from a prior experience to anything that feels similar, even if they intellectually know that this person is safe.

Both wanted desperately to be able to share touch that feels good. After all, the ultimate recovery after an assault is to feel safe enough in the body again to feel pleasure—to reclaim pleasure on their own terms.

After I described the bodyful touch practice to them during their third session, I invited them to share their feelings and thoughts about the practice before beginning. "We don't even have to do this practice today," I made sure to tell them. Sarah was visibly uncomfortable, rubbing her hands and tapping her feet on the floor, and Emily was visibly rigid in her torso, her eyes fixed on Sarah, scanning her for information. "I don't want all the attention on me," Sarah began, "I feel like you're just waiting for me to change." Emily's brow lifted in the middle of her forehead, visibly empathetic. "I don't want you to change—I just want you to enjoy being near me so you can be more of who you are." I encouraged Emily to tell Sarah, "I trust your body autonomy." Sarah blinked and then asked her to repeat the phrase. More clearly this time, Emily said, "I trust your body autonomy, Sarah." Sarah softened in her seat, and I asked her what she noticed. "I feel like I want to lean toward her a bit." I encouraged her to follow this movement impulse. She shifted her body a few inches closer to

Emily, and Emily, in her excitement, reached for Sarah, causing her to pause. "Too much, too fast," Sarah quickly said. I encouraged Emily to breathe into her back body, slowing her awareness around her excitement, her arousal. Once her shoulders softened and her eyes relaxed into their sockets again, smoothing the muscles around her eyes, I encouraged her to say the body autonomy phrase again. Sarah gave a small, rueful laugh. I asked her what she noticed. "It's her arousal. That pace is scary to me. I'm not sure what will happen, if I'll dissociate and not be able to ask her to slow down or stop. Then I'll be vulnerable and feel a bunch of shame again." Emily settled into her seat a bit more and said, "That makes so much sense to me." We then took the rest of the session to explore pacing of movement in the rhythm of arousal, encouraging them to slow down and for Emily to not be taken over by the momentum of arousal until she and Sarah were attuned with a similar pace. Sarah talked about feeling so much relief that she was not the only one keeping track of this now. She knows that Emily's arousal is a positive thing and doesn't want her to suppress it—she just wants her to slow down and be assured that Emily is conscious in the altered state of arousal. Some of her vigilance could finally soften, and exploring touch was beginning to feel interesting.

As a clinician, I find that this kind of moment is a golden opportunity, and not just for the person with a difficult touch history. When both partners agree to dedicate themselves to a quality of touch that comes from an awake attention with their somatic aliveness in order to heal a partner's relationship with touch, the partner who is mostly comfortable with touch can learn more about their own experience, their impact, the pace and rhythm of their arousal, and what touch truly means to them. They get to savor the magic of intimate contact that is fully consensual, fully felt, and fully received. Both partners benefit from learning what kind of touch generates aliveness and what kind of touch takes them out of their body and out of the present moment.

During this exploration, many people, both high and low-touch, find that they have been overriding an inner "no" to certain kinds of contact in order to maintain a relationship or keep themselves safe. This is a worthy exploration because, when touch doesn't feel pleasurable or safe enough, body armor in the form of tension in the muscles and tissues hardens, and we don't get access to all the emotional, relational, and physiological benefits. The hardening of body armor increases the reflex of retraction from the touch of a partner, communicating a lack of trust or safety. This is their body saying "no" to the unsafe feeling, not necessarily saying "no" to the intimate partner. Regardless, for the partner who is the recipient of this retraction, they can begin to question (or defend against) the feeling that they themselves are unsafe. This creates such a difficult dynamic for partners, both within themselves and between the partners, when intellectually they might know that touch between them is safe enough, but their bodies are reacting as though it is not. This incongruence is confusing and challenging to address.

Fortunately, relationship with touch can be rewired. One of the most powerful relationship-impacting skills that you can learn as an intimate partner is an intentional touch practice that can help you learn how to attune with yourself, then with a partner, and heal any prior non-consensual experiences.

An intentional touch practice can help you learn more about yourself, to understand where you are touching from within your inner emotional landscape as you identify the origin and intention of the touch that you are expressing. Combine this understanding with embodied communication, and your partner gets to experience your congruent self, allowing their nervous system and vigilant mind to relax. Through *movement sequencing from core connectivity*, you get to learn if you are touching from a place of stress or anxiousness within you, looking for comfort, touching from a place of obligation, or if you are feeling connected with your partner and are touching from a place of mutual resonance.

Whether you find that you are connecting from a place of anxiousness, a performative expectation, or excitement, and you are not aware of your partner's interest, connect with your own body first. This is a solo intentional transition like the practice that I described in Chapter 3.

Solo Intentional Transition: *Place your hands on your body, such as over your heart and solar plexus, and find your out-breath to settle your nervous system. Ask your body what it needs to soften the anxiousness, to settle into a more present-moment awake state, and follow the movement impulse. Perhaps you could continue to focus on your out-breath, inviting a whole-body shimmy to shake out tension. Perhaps you could use your palm to gently tap your chest, dislodging tightness, or massage the muscles and tissues of your chest, just below the collarbone, to bring your mind into focus. Once you attune with your own body, then you can turn to your partner, begin with stillness touch, and find your flow in connection. We will continue with this practice in the next section.*

Educating yourself about touch, exploring together with embodied consent, and sharing your honest experience is an often-overlooked skill that supports the relationship, preventing the accumulation of resentment or misunderstanding. In order to have an effective learning experience, this process has five primary things to consider:

1. Consider the context: Is the immediate environment comfortable? Do you have an ample amount of time to explore and you're not in a rush? Do you have initial embodied consent to explore with a partner?
2. Attune to self first: What is your nervous system state? What does your body need to feel more comfortable and more present? What are you hoping for? Any expectations of how the touch experience might go? Identify expectations and agendas and set them aside.

3. Check in with each other: Share how you both are feeling, what the space needs for you to be more comfortable, and the expectations you have set aside.
4. Bodyful touch practice: Guided practice that I will detail in the following.
5. Share experience for learning and integration: Share how your body was impacted by giving or receiving touch. At what points did you feel your body relax? What touch qualities did you enjoy?

Guided Bodyful Touch Practice

After considering the context, choose who will receive touch first.

The person receiving touch turns their attention inward to listen to their internal landscape, expanding the body on the in-breath and settling into a yield on the out-breath. Ask your body what area of your body would feel safe enough and interesting to receive contact today in this particular context. When you are first learning this practice, make sure that you choose a non-central arousal anatomy area to explore. I only recommend applying this practice to central arousal anatomy once you are more familiar with the practice and feeling full embodied consent to explore beyond peripheral arousal anatomy. Once your body tells you what area would enjoy contact—this could be a large area like your back or a smaller area like your fingers—let your partner know, "My body feels safe enough and interested to receive contact here today."

For the partner offering contact, your partner has just requested contact! Take a moment to breathe in their request and how their request feels in your body. Pause here to feel that, with this request, *contact has already been made*. Not physically yet, but the request for touch will generate a ripple of sensation through your somatic landscape. This is a form of touch, a transition into connection that is beginning to create the environment for touch to be embodied and enjoyed. So, decelerate around the impulse to jump right in and let the initial sensations fill you up, breathing into your back body and front body. The rhythm of breath and the awareness of your whole body will allow containment of the sensations and any arousal that is present so that it can circulate without spilling over or shutting down. Centering yourself around the inner sensation also identifies the somatic location from which to *sequence* your movement.

For both partners, engage your *breath support*. On your in-breath, expand your ribcage and belly, and on your out-breath, softening muscle and bone, allowing any micromovements to happen that help you settle in—a soft shimmy, a shifting of your seat, or a stretch. On your next in-breath, breathe into your back body and pelvis, widening your hips over your seat on your out-breath.

For the one offering touch, feel the somatic sensation from the request and ask your body how it feels about this beloved person requesting contact. Study the sensation for its texture, shape, and movement quality. All sensations have a movement quality to them—the sensation of excitement is often a fast tingling or vibration that lifts you up from within, while the sensation of relaxation is often a melting or settling that widens at the bottom. Then, surround this sensation with breath, inviting it to amplify and spread down your arms into your hands and fingers. Allow your body to express the movement quality of this sensation as you shift your position to be comfortable and allow ease of movement, engaging your head–tail connection for dynamic alignment, finding stability in mobility. Remember that touch that comes from an uncomfortable, rigid, or off-balance body will feel equally uncomfortable, so continue to oscillate your awareness between what you are feeling in your body and what you are sensing from your partner.

Now, in your own time, breathe the inner sensation into your hands and sequence your movement inch by inch from the sensation to reach out and place your hand on your partner's body where they invited you. Begin with *stillness touch*, allowing your hand to land on your partner's body, letting gravity determine the pressure and how your hands contour over the area. Allow both of your bodies to yield, full in-breath and full out-breath.

It is with *stillness touch* that consent can be felt, and attunement can begin. Slow your awareness to feel your partner's in-breath and out-breath, and feel the pulse in your fingers aligning with the pulse from their skin. For the partner receiving touch, breathe into the place where your partner's hand is contacting you, volumizing and expanding your body as though your skin could touch them back. And on your out-breath, let your body invite their hand to come with you.

Once the attunement of breath and the yield in the body is felt by both partners, the partner offering touch can begin *moving touch*, allowing their hand or hands to be fascinated by the contour of their partner's body area, the landscape of muscle and bone, the warmth of their partner's skin, and the give of the muscles as they gently press in. This is the body of your beloved, and making contact like this is an honor, a privilege, and a gateway into deeper bonding. As you explore this area of your partner's body, make sure that you don't go outside the invited area at this time (we will discuss this more later), and continue to oscillate your attention between your experience of your own body and the responsiveness of the body of your partner receiving your touch. When you oscillate into your own body, notice how you are feeling, making sure that you are comfortable and keeping track of your own body sensations. If you are having trouble oscillating, engage your *dynamic alignment* as you shift your head–tail connection to gently lean forward and then, breathing into your back body, gently leaning back, and then returning to your midline as you center yourself.

Ask yourself these questions:

- From where within me is my touch originating from?
- Is my body comfortable? Do I feel grounded?
- Am I having thoughts? Dislodge your attention from thoughts and return to the body-to-body connection and rhythm.

When you check in with your partner's body, ask yourself these questions:

- Are they taking full breaths?
- Are their muscles retracting away from my hand or expanding and leaning into me?

If you are unsure how your partner is feeling, ask them! You don't have to read their mind. Agree to continue the secure attachment practice of direct embodied communication and, once a partner has shared, tell them *thank you for telling me.*

For the partner receiving touch, you are also practicing oscillation. Notice how your body is feeling receiving this touch and the ripples of sensation. Notice the movement quality of the sensation that you feel and allow your body to slowly and intentionally express this movement quality in response to your partner's touch. Allow your body to be moved by the rhythm of their hand. For example, when they gently press into your muscles, allow your body to soften, and as they move their hand one way or the other, allow your body to move in the direction that their hand is guiding you. Practice staying in contact with each other as these micro-movements happen.

After the partner offering touch has explored the invited area of their partner's body for a little while (you determine how long, but I usually have people start with five minutes), bring your hands back to *stillness touch* on your partner's body. Invite another full in-breath and out-breath as you breathe gratitude through your hands into your partner's body. Then bring your hands back to your body, and both of you can notice how it feels to have contact come to a close. Are you ready for the touch to conclude, or do you miss your partner's hands?

Turn your bodies toward each other to begin the sharing part of the practice. Take a moment to notice how it feels to see your partner after the contact and/or sense the impact of sitting facing each other. You could even take notes first in a journal to remember the important details and guide your sharing. Use sensation words directly from the place that you feel them in your body. Remember that awareness on the level of sensation supports activating those deeper brain structures to create change in the nervous system. And using sensation words and sensation-sourced movements helps your partner to feel you more deeply. Offer grace to each other here because this level of sharing can be quite vulnerable.

Here is a structure to use initially—and then over time add your own language to personalize your sharing. Using embodied communication, begin by thanking each other for investing the time to explore together, and then take turns sharing what you noticed. Say, *when your hands were exploring x, y, z (insert the area of your body here), I noticed that I felt x,y,z (tingling, melting relaxation, arousal bubbling up from my pelvis, etc.).* Once you share what you noticed, let your partner know that you feel complete in your sharing for the moment and invite your partner to share.

Mutual Bodyful Touch Practice

Once you have practiced the one-way bodyful touch practice and feel familiar with the steps, begin to practice a mutual bodyful touch practice where you are both contacting each other, alternating touch and response. This creates a flow of call and response, weaving touch, breath, and movement.

Begin with self-attunement—full breath in, long breath out, noticing sensations and their movement qualities, asking what is needed to help your body settle into the present-moment awareness. Invite your body to move any stretches, shimmies, movements, and audible out-breaths to soften muscle and bone, feeling the impact of gravity over time. Notice as these sensation echoes move through your body and, checking back in with the original area of sensation, notice if you feel the same or different.

Turn to face your partner and share what you notice in your body as you settle in—what sensation echoes your body brought into the space, what moved through, and what you notice now. Thank your partner for sharing their experience, and then check in about what area of your body you want to begin contact. Perhaps you want to lean shoulders into each other, begin with palms together, or backs together.

Begin with your one point of contact. Let's use the example of palms together for ease of guidance. Invite an in-breath and as you breathe out, connect your palm with your partner's palm with stillness touch. As you settle into initial contact, breathe into your body and notice emergent sensations in your inner landscape. Breathe into your back body, widen your hips, and bring your awareness back to the points of contact between your palm and the palm of your partner. Notice the temperature, pressure, and micro movements that happen in stillness.

Once your bodies settle in, one of you can initiate a movement in response to the contact. Perhaps one of you presses your palm more firmly into your partner's hand. Partner, receive the firmer pressure, allowing your hand to respond by slowly moving backward without losing contact, and then follow your next movement impulse. Perhaps your impulse is to gently press back or to roll your palm toward you, pressing the back of your hand to your partner's palm. Pause in stillness and take a breath, oscillating awareness to your inner landscape, asking *where within myself am I touching from?*, then to the connection between you, then to noticing your partner, sensing the quality of their presence. Then begin again following movement impulse, allowing your partner to receive the movement and respond with their movement impulse.

Continue to explore this way for about five minutes or until you experience a moment of *flow* between you, where it feels as though there is no beginning or ending to your movement exchange. Then bring your movements back to stillness contact, and then back to your own body. Turn to each other and share what you noticed. Here are some questions to explore together:

- At what point did you feel most grounded in the contact? What were the somatic sensations and movement qualities that happened when feeling grounded?
- At what point did you feel confident in following your own movement impulse or responding to your partner's movement impulse? What were the somatic sensations and movement qualities that happened when feeling confident?
- At what point did you feel unsure about where your partner was guiding you or where you were guiding your partner? What were the somatic sensations and movement qualities that happened when feeling unsure?
- What was helpful for you in transitioning from feeling unsure back into feeling grounded or in the flow with your partner?

Incorporating Central Arousal Anatomy

Now that you have explored one-way bodyful touch, mutual bodyful touch, and hopefully found some flow with each other, you can consider incorporating central arousal anatomy (clothed and then unclothed, fully or partially—you get to choose!) into the bodyful touch practice with your intimate partner. Be clear with each other that you are interested and ready to move to this step before beginning this practice. When doing this practice together, make the agreement that the touch that you explore is the intention and that you will not make the jump into mutual sexual intimacy at this time. Containing the experience to a simple touch will help you to stay in the present moment and not switch into anticipation or defense toward what will happen next. If you like, schedule a sexy-time date for a different time and day.

Also, revisit your embodied consent practice and remind each other that this is a moment-to-moment awareness of yes, no, and arousal nonconcordance. No expectations. Embrace the process and be open to shifting as needed by engaging the movement fundamental principles of breath support and dynamic alignment to keep your aliveness and flexibility online.

Begin by tending to the context, adjusting the environment to be comfortable for both of you and free of distractions—whatever supports your nervous system to settle into a relaxed and receptive state.

Once the context is set, turn your attention inward with the full in-breath and long out-breath, supporting your body to expand and then release through any movement or stretch impulses that begin to happen. Explore the emergent sensations in your inner landscape, what they want you to know or are trying to do for you in this moment. In-breath and out-breath. What is needed to land in the space more fully? Then, ask yourself if you want to offer or receive touch first, as this will be a one-way bodyful practice initially. Share with each other your preference and decide who will offer and who will receive.

If you are receiving, let your intimate partner know the area of your central arousal anatomy where you feel safe enough and interested to receive bodyful touch, as well as an area of your peripheral arousal anatomy for touch to begin, that is, hands, back, legs, and so on. You may also choose to have clothing on or off, depending on your feelings of embodied consent. Trust your pacing.

If you are offering touch, take a few moments of full breath, breathing into your back body, finding a comfortable position, and circulating any arousal energy you may be feeling. In-breath and out-breath. Notice how you feel about this beloved partner and the emergent sensations as you do this. Slowly, when you are ready, place your hands on the invited peripheral arousal anatomy place in stillness touch. This is a moment to say hello to your partner's body, give them an opportunity to receive your touch, and let the nervous system settle. In-breath and out-breath. Let any movement impulses sequence through your bodies—a shimmy, a stretch, and an audible out-breath. When both of you share a readiness to progress, the offering partner shifts their hands to the invited area of their partner's central arousal anatomy, allowing your hand or hands to settle on their body in stillness touch with gravity, determining the pressure over the contour of the area.

While hands are in stillness touch, the partner who is receiving touch breathes into the area contacted by their partner's hands. Remember the movement qualities of arousal anatomy and how these softer tissues containing erectile tissue have the ability to expand as they engorge with blood, oxygen, and a sensation of pleasure. As the receiver breathes into this area of their arousal anatomy, they can expand the area with their breath, softening their body on the out-breath. Take your time here! Learning together how the movement of arousal anatomy begins on its own without direct, purposeful stimulation is an opportunity to share in the intimate knowing your own body and the body of your partner.

If this is your first time with this level of bodyful touch practice, you can bring the practice to a close here after a short period of time. If this is not your first time and both the partner offering and the partner receiving are interested in exploring movement, you can continue here.

Once you both have experienced the receiving partner's arousal anatomy responding with movement, expansion, and engorgement, breath is in full expression (not restricted), and embodied consent is expressed, the offering partner can begin movement of their hand. Remember to maintain skin-to-skin contact with your hand as you move and explore—rubbing a hand over these areas can feel uncomfortable and create unwanted friction with the soft tissues. Allow yourself to be so fascinated by the temperature of their skin, the feeling of deeper arousal, the anatomy structures below the skin, and the contour of their body. Breathe into your hand(s) a sense of honoring this body, loving this body, and appreciating the journey that this body has been on.

If you are the partner receiving contact, breathe in this feeling of love, of honoring, of appreciation into your body, acknowledging the magnificence of your body, its miraculous capabilities to feel, move, receive, and to experience pleasure and resilience. This is the magic of being in a body.

After about five minutes, the offering partner brings their hand movement back to stillness touch, and then back to their own body. Turn to each other, find each other's eyes if that feels accessible, share gratitude, and share your experience:

- What was your experience of stillness touch on your peripheral arousal anatomy?
- What happened for you as you felt your partner's hands shift from peripheral to central arousal anatomy?
- What sensations did you notice as your arousal anatomy expressed any kind of movement?
- What happened for you as your partner breathed love, honoring, and appreciation into your arousal anatomy?

In future sessions, you can try mutual bodyful touch with arousal anatomy and, hopefully, incorporate this quality of touch into your sexual intimacy with each other.

Create Shared Touch Values

After gathering your learning from your bodyful touch experiences, you can begin to create your *shared values* related to touch. Shared values could look like any of these:

- We prioritize slowness to attune through our different desire styles.
- We value honesty even when it's not what we want to hear so that we feel congruence with each other to build trust.

- We emphasize embodied consent moment to moment to support partner A's history of unsafe touch.
- We value checking in emotionally first before engaging in touch to feel more grounded in each other's presence.

Having a shared value related to touch gives you a sense of common purpose and shared meaningfulness. These are guiding lights when a challenge appears because they make it worth the present moment discomfort or distress that can arise—investing in touch is now in service of a greater, shared purpose, allowing grace and compassion when pre-effort movements happen within the learning experience (see Chapter 2 for an explanation about pre-effort).

This one experience is just the beginning of a journey of gathering data to understand your shared values—revisit this practice in different contexts, at different times of the week or day, and over time as your relationship progresses through the years and through challenging life events. Let your shared touch values be living, breathing, transforming guides.

Practicing this sequence of attuning to self, then attuning with each other, checking in, appreciating each other for sharing, managing distress, and reconnecting with ownership of your own experience and expression, followed by sharing gratitude, is an important rhythm of having a secure attachment structure in your relationship.

12

YOUR INTIMATE DYNAMIC

Erotic Mapping for Resilience

By now, you probably realize that sensation and movement are not standalone monuments of experience, but dynamic expressions of your body revealing the impact of your life journey—overlapping waves of development and learning, where the former waves influence the latter, and you are a culmination-in-motion of it all. Noticing you're in-the-moment landscape of somatic sensations is not an event unto itself—it is an echo of where you have been and an indication of where you are going, a whole arc of experience with past, present, and future existing at the same time. This is where vital information exists about how your body can be actively supported to shift from defensive to receptive, from dysregulated to regulated, and from happy to full-body joyful, meanwhile rewriting old, limiting movement patterns in exchange for more congruent and broader expression.

The process of visiting moments of difficulty and rewriting motor plans that diminish your aliveness allows you to update the way you feel in your body as well as your beliefs about yourself and what you think is possible in your relationship. Your brilliant nervous system has a built-in editing department, ready to identify current patterns and expressions that have collapsed all movement options into a specific phrase, in order to expand your movement repertoire once again to find the expression that better fits the moment. You are not at the mercy of your prior experiences and your current nervous system state—you have the ability to be in an active relationship with your responses and with the way you engage with your intimate partner to optimize your intimate interactions.

You also realize by now that how you inhabit your body and express your inner experience impacts your intimate partner in ways that can affirm your affinity for each other or create distance between you (and everything along

DOI: 10.4324/9781003508984-16

that continuum between). Any meaningful moment between the two of you can be explored through as a dynamic system of movement phrases—a combined arc of expression—to find the interplay between you and your intimate partner in important contexts. This is how you can identify and gain insight into your body-to-body relationship to actively shift from challenge and misattunement toward mutual enjoyment and embodied attunement.

The process that I have developed to do this effectively is called *erotic mapping.*

Erotic mapping is a *somatic creative process* that guides you and your partner to identify each of your movement profiles (discussed in Chapter 9, *Rhythm of Attunement*) for (1) when you experience a *challenge* in your intimacy, (2) when you are feeling *resourced*, easeful, and excited in your sexuality so that you can learn to access your *resilience* movements to stay within your window of capacity with each other and not get lost in dysregulation and/or conflict, and (3) when you find yourself in the shadow, which then causes you drop into *autopilot* reactions which relieve the tension for the moment but are not inherently nourishing.

It is within this present-moment movement phrasing that you can find the congruent ways that you express, which supports attunement with your partner, as well as the discordant patterns that developed from an earlier emotional wound or missed developmental step, adding challenge to your dynamic.

Let's take a closer look at this bodyful practice that gives you a way to put your skills of relational attunement and your awareness of your own movement expression into usable action.

Erotic Mapping Practice

I call this specifically an *erotic* mapping practice because working through challenges together toward attunement and pleasure has the strong potential of being, well, *erotic.* To feel the rhythm of tension and release, to feel both safe enough and push your edges at the same time, and to challenge each other and work together to navigate through an obstacle and land in relief and excitement into a new way of relating—this is a recipe for eroticism. And the culmination of the practice is to find yourselves in a place of genuine mutual pleasure and shared meaningfulness. It is compelling—an emotionally, psychologically, and somatically verdant territory.

The mapping process involves identifying three main areas of your relationship to explore your combined movement expression in each: *Resource, Challenge, and Shadow* (see Figure 12.1). These are the primary colors on your erotic mapping wheel—your red, yellow, and blue. By bringing these three movement expressions together into a movement phrase, you get to see the non-verbal relationship between you play out in real time with the

Figure 12.1 The Erotic Map.

content of the story in the background. By putting the verbal dialogue on the backburner and allowing the somatic story to play out moment-to-moment, you can more easily gain insights into what is essentially happening between you, and present new options to better relate.

The overlapped areas show you how you transition between the main three areas of the map. The overlapped areas are *Resilience, Dysregulation,* and *Autopilot.* These are the secondary colors of your erotic mapping wheel, where two primary realms are bridged together—your orange, green, and violet. Remember how the nervous system doesn't just snap in and out of states but requires transition time to shift states? These overlapped areas on the map give us a glimpse of what is happening for you as you transition between resource and challenge, challenge and shadow, shadow and resource.

Embodied attunement begins before you even touch by sensing each other's somatic presence and movement expression, and the erotic mapping process gives you a clear process to find your pathway, together. By getting to know how you embody your sexuality resource together—you identify the somatic markers (meaningful movement qualities) and learn to enhance expression through total body connectivity principles—it becomes a place to intentionally return in a challenging moment. The *embodied simulation* (Gallese, 2004) mechanism, allowing your body to see, hear, and feel your partner's internal experience, gives you insight into your impact on your partner as well as what might be a better way to approach them. The more present-moment embodied you are, the more likely you are to find and maintain intimate attunement. Erotic mapping practice allows you to explore what is needed to find balance and flow with different movement profiles, different desire styles, and different paces of arousal. Rhythmic entrainment fosters nervous system coherence and resonance, so let's incorporate all of the movement fundamentals as you explore your map.

Let's explore each realm on the map so that you can create your own. Take out your journal or a large piece of paper and draw the three overlapping circles as you see in the image above. You will fill each area in as we go.

Let's begin.

Resource: The area of resource, the upper left-hand circle on the map, is where you get to identify the context in which your connection is a *resource* as you discover where your emotional and physical intimate connection feels easeful and exciting. This is your full-body effort expression where you are masterful—fully coordinated in your movement where your ability meets the demands of the activity with skillfulness.

First things first—identifying your strengths first gives you a good foundation to return to after a rupture or intimate difficulty is explored in the challenge area.

When exploring resource, visualize what you really enjoy doing together. This could be anything—your Sunday morning pickleball game, your Friday night movie night on the couch together, your weekly ballroom dance class, or your hotel sexy-time (no dishes or laundry!)—any activity where you feel great in your body and also feel connected with each other.

As you visualize this activity that you love to do together, visit the guidance of movement fundamentals and make notes as you go. Engage breath support with a full in-breath and a long out-breath, expanding and yielding into your body. Breathe around the sensations that you notice, giving them the space and support they need to move within as you describe them as descriptively as possible—texture, temperature, size/shape, levels of muscle tension.

Then move on to sequencing your movement by first finding the inner movement impulse of the sensation. Does the movement impulse have a light or rising quality, a spreading and widening quality, or a heavy, weighted quality to it? Does the sensation have a slow or quick pace, or does it gradually build in speed, bursting through to then slow again? And does it have more of an indulging rhythmic quality to it, swaying or twisting, or do you feel more of a fighting rhythmic quality, jumping or bubbling?

What shape is your body making in space? Is your body shaping itself by growing or shrinking, elongating or shortening, hollowing or rounding in a particular direction?

As you sequence the movement from the core of the sensation through the rest of your torso and limbs and head, see if you can engage dynamic alignment, allowing your body to adjust as needed to see the movement all the way through with intention through the space within your kinesphere. Remember that these can be small micromovements or larger macromovement expressions. Also, you are not necessarily expressing the movement of the activity itself (if it's jogging together, you won't necessarily be jogging in place for your movement); you are expressing the feeling within your body *that you have* while *doing the activity.*

Now, ask yourself these questions:

- What qualities of your movement do you notice here?
- What happens to you when you share this movement with your partner? Remember to witness each other with compassion and interest and thank your partner for sharing their movement with you.
- If it feels safe enough and also interesting, ask your partner to mirror your movement. Partner, remember that you are mirroring by finding the movement quality in your own body versus mimicking or trying to copy your partner's movement exactly. What happens to you when your partner mirrors your movement? Does your movement stay the same or change slightly?
- Try sharing both of your movements at the same time. Remember breath support here. Allow yourself to be fascinated by how similar your movements are or how different they may be—this is how your partner feels inside when you engage in a fun and meaningful activity together! Isn't that interesting! You may notice that your movements begin to change a bit as you share with each other. Let this happen! You are beginning to find your combined resource movement. Make notes about how your movements shift into a co-created phrase. Shift your awareness into the panoramic, taking it all in at once. This will also help you get out of the concern about doing it right or wrong that can happen with a fixated focused attention.
- Share with each other what you noticed during this exploration.

Make note of your shared activity (hopefully you can list more than one!) and write descriptive words for your sensations and movement qualities on your combined map. This is the foundation you will come back to after visiting your challenge.

Challenge: The upper right-hand circle of the map is where the challenge sits. This is the place where your intimacy feels difficult at times: your desire difference, anxiousness leading up to intimacy, feeling of disconnection after sex where integration should be, body pain from a chronic condition, or arousal non-concordance when your partner is asking you for what you want (just to name a few options).

Challenge is where you want to be in tune with your partner, but you have such a hard time getting there because there seem to be so many obstacles in the way. Still within your window of capacity, you are able to feel the anxiousness, embarrassment, discomfort, or pain. This is the area of pre-effort (learning and/or defending) where you probably find yourself more often in a defensive nervous system state, uncoordinated or minimized in your movement expression, as you find yourself more hesitant with more abrupt or straining movements. Old, discordant movement patterns emerge here. Muscle tension increases with bound-tension flow, restricting breath and diminishing movement capacity. Your pre-effort motor pattern puts a stopper in creativity by inhibiting whole-body connectivity and whole-brain function—the brain has neurocepted potential danger, activating protective body armor. You begin to feel shaky with anxiousness or fear, you feel floaty and disconnected as you start to dissociate, or you sense your body heading into shut-down with a wall of tension across your chest.

This discordant pattern could be the result of an early attachment wound where a caregiver, important family member, or peers did not attune to you or were unpredictable in their behavior, or were scary or shaming at times. This is the body memory of a child who adapted to an adverse environmental or relationship condition that becomes a part of the relational field. Somatic Psychotherapist Ruella Frank says that, when the body adapts a response from an adverse childhood experience:

> *The poorly coordinated pattern is internalized and integrated in the nervous system of the child, meaning that it is made part of the whole, but is not assimilated or taken into the system in a way that produces harmony. That is, the discordant pattern will come to dominate the system, and to overpower the preceding pattern as well as the subsequent pattern that emerges.*
>
> (Frank, p. 48)

Your discordant, defensive pattern could also be the result of an earlier relationship wound, which often happens during a pre-effort relationship stage or transition time, where attunement was difficult and when you didn't have the skills or nervous system capacity to deal with the unknown. Everyone goes through this at some point—life is challenging like that. Because you were not able to meet each other or you were unable to support your partner, body armor was activated, and a coping mechanism, or defensive movement pattern, was developed instead.

Fear, anxiety, anger, resentment, and hurt can all collapse possible movement pattern responses into just a few limited pathways—fight, flight, freeze, or fawn.

The first and most important thing to do while exploring your challenge realm is to thank your body for trying to protect you. The context and environmental conditions were too big to handle, and you were not supported enough in that moment to make a different choice. In other words, you did the best you could with what you had at the time.

I encourage you to breathe in gratitude into your body for doing its best and notice, once you do this, does the sensation within feel the same or different? Finding compassion for yourself and your partner is the first step to shifting from a defensive pre-effort state into a safe-enough, *learning*, pre-effort state. Get curious about what this movement pattern is trying to do, albeit unsuccessfully or non-relationally, so that you can engage the movement fundamentals and find your way out. Ask your body, what does it need to feel safe enough to soften and begin to sequence your movement into more of your kinesphere?

By establishing a safe-enough environment—actively connecting with your own body, sharing congruent and embodied communication, then both of you telling your partner what genuinely makes sense about why their body is expressing that defensive pattern, and offering them a gratitude for sharing something so vulnerable—you'll be able to bring your whole brain back online to say, "you know what, it's time for a do-over!" This is what will allow you to find that breath support around the challenging sensations and begin to soften and open your body and to invite more flow into your muscles.

As you connect the challenge movement phrase with the resilience movement phrase using this somatic creative process, you can open up those possible movement pathways again, broadening your repertoire of responses. This is where you can access that first overlapping bridge between challenge and resource—the bridge of *resilience*. Your resilience is your ability to identify that you have become activated and discover what your body needs to get back to Resource on your erotic map. Find your out-breath. Engage a ragdoll-like shaking to meet the intensity of the discomfort and let it tumble out of you. Drop your chin to your chest and use your hands to pat your chest or squeeze your arms. Place an ice pack on your body for a few minutes (this activates your parasympathetic nervous system). Go for a brisk walk to get your heart rate up and then rest while focusing on your out-breath (these are T.I.P.P. skills from Dialectical Behavior Therapy that help you regulate your nervous system quickly and efficiently).

Take your time with the resilience bridge to really learn what is helpful to release the bound muscle tension and dysregulation, and support each other to take the time you both need. Always use "I" or "we" language when inviting the use of the resilience bridge—no one likes to be told to be the one to chill out. This is an opportunity to invite a shared value of caring for yourselves. Say something like, "I'm feeling too activated to work through this right now so I'm going to activate my resilience bridge. Let's take the time to regulate and then come back to talk about the challenge because this is important." Remember to *regulate, not ruminate,* during the time out. Don't forget to tell your partner that you want to reconnect and continue the process because they are important, and this process is important. This is what I like to call the *intentional time-out.*

This is why exploring challenge in the erotic mapping process is helpful—you are not in the heat of the moment of the actual challenge, and therefore, you are less likely to get as activated, so you can stay awake, aware, and accessing whole-brain creativity to find resilience and bridge back to your resource movement pattern together.

If you are not in a safe-enough space and the context is too overstimulating and uncomfortable when challenge presents itself, you may begin to drop into the bridge between challenge and shadow—the bridge of *dysregulation*. Instead of softening, your muscles further tighten, and you begin to shut down, dissociate, or raise your voice in blaming, defensive statements. At this point, you are too dysregulated and would benefit from taking an intentional time out to access your resilience bridge on your own first before reconnecting with each other. Shadow is beginning to overtake you. This is an opportunity to practice secure attachment with yourselves. All of us get dysregulated sometimes. Taking the time to validate ourselves and care for ourselves is about embracing our humanness, owning our own reactions as something that has protected us, and learning to shift out of dysregulated reactions using your somatic skills.

Before we explore the shadow realm, let me guide you through the challenge part of the map.

Consider what feels challenging for you in your intimacy. Remember that the structure of your body can hold you here—you won't fall apart. Trust that your body will share with you what you need to return to a grounded place.

As you visualize your challenge (desire difference, chronic pain impacting intimacy, etc.), notice the sensations that begin to happen in your body. Do you notice your posture changing as your body shapes itself in growing or shrinking movements, hollowing or bulging from your chest or the middle of your back? Are you expressing more of an indulgent rhythm or a fighting rhythm? Do you notice your pace has quickened or slowed down? This could feel sudden or gradual. Do you notice more bound tension-flow in your muscles, or does it seem that your body has lost all tone and is feeling neutral, lacking any tension or release?

Exaggerate your movement just a bit. Remember to anchor yourself with your out-breath or a resource outside yourself in the room. Get a drink of water or hug a pillow, and then return to the challenge movement profile, oscillating between your challenge and your anchor as needed. What does your body want you to know here? Take your time and make some notes of your sensations and movement qualities using descriptive words.

Now, find your resilience bridge movements. Out-breath. Ice pack. Shaking. Squeeze your arms or pat your chest. You've got this. Slowly, return to your resource movement from before and notice, does the resource movement feel the same or different? Your resource movement may feel different—deeper, more lush, or more relieving. You may have tears here.

This is worthy work. As is said in Stoic philosophy, "the obstacle becomes the way."

Now, ask yourself these questions:

- What qualities of your movement do you notice here?
- What happens to you when you share this movement with your partner? Remember to witness each other with compassion and interest and thank your partner for sharing their movement with you.
- Try sharing both of your movements at the same time. Allow yourself to breathe into your back body and widen your focus to take your partner in with compassion. Are your movements similar or are they different?—this is how your partner feels inside when they are experiencing a challenge.
- Notice, where does this feel familiar from? Earlier in life, earlier in your relationship?
- What happens within your own body as you witness your partner?
- What do you need to soften toward your partner?
- What makes sense about why they may be feeling this? What do you know about them? Their history, their values?
- Share with each other what you noticed during this exploration with kindness, curiosity, and compassion for each other's humanness.

The better you get to know how challenge shows up in your body, the better you will be able to identify when you are there and wake yourself up from the descent into the abyss of dysregulation. Your partner cannot regulate you or own your reactions—only you can regulate yourself to return to your window of capacity in order to share your difficult feelings. Then you can share observations, make requests, and reconnect.

Shadow: The bottom circle of the erotic map is where you have arrived in shadow, and you are no longer in the present moment. Your nervous system activation has hit play on those old tapes in your mind where you are assuming the worst of your partner and of yourself. In these dysregulated movements, you have forgotten about the times that you and your partner have supported each other, felt attuned, or worked through a disagreement.

Shadow usually sounds something like: "I'll never get what I need." "I can't fully express myself because I'm too much." "I'm not enough for my partner." "My partner doesn't care about me." Notice how these statements use absolute, polarizing language. These statements are rigid and unyielding, just as are the movements that accompany these thoughts. These are thoughts and beliefs that developed from difficult moments in your younger-hood from your parents, caregivers, peers, and community, and your body developed a way of organizing itself to protect against the awful impact that these kinds of beliefs make. No one gets out of childhood without shadow because difficulty is a part of growing up.

Within the shadow is also the *golden shadow.* The golden shadow, a Jungian psychology term, is full of your best and brightest qualities that you siloed off for safekeeping because you felt criticized, minimized, rejected, or unseen in your creativity, your emotional expression, your confidence, or your ambition by people in your early life. By exploring the somatic expression of your shadow and accessing resilience, you can recover your brilliant potential and integrate it into the whole of who you are. This is why many people shrink when complimented or invited to share their brilliance. Because it is in the shadow, being recognized or invited to shine can feel deeply uncomfortable and dysregulating.

One thing for sure is we can't stay in the shadow for long—it is often too painful and disorienting. This is when the *autopilot* bridge takes over to save you from your immediate discomfort, offering just enough resource to get out of the sting of pain—but you are not quite awake yet. Instead, you are scrolling your phone, continuing to eat though you are not hungry, turning on yet another show to binge watch or yet another porn video, using a substance, or falling asleep. This will not heal your heart—it is a compulsive reaction—but it will take the pain away for a moment because you are distracted, stuck in the reach-and-grasp part of the satisfaction cycle without any yield because there is no nourishment here to take in. The nervous system is smart. Your body knows how to distract you to get you to look away when you are out of emotional energy, you don't currently have the skills to tackle the challenge, or your environment does not support a safe-enough space to access a truly restorative resource.

The goal here is not to rid yourself of all autopilot reactions (though it is important to replace the more harmful ones like substance abuse or self-harming behaviors) because you need them from time to time as a reprieve and loading screen. The goal is to find ways to wake up within your autopilot reaction, allowing you to take a breath and intentionally walk your way across the resilience bridge toward resource, nourishment, and connection.

Take a few minutes here to visualize what happens when you've arrived at a challenge and get too dysregulated. Do you find you sharply pull away from your partner and say, "I'll just do it all myself!," I don't care anymore," or "I can't do this." Do you grasp at your partner in fear of being left, ready to do anything to change, to fix, to suppress, or to tolerate? Notice the muscle tension, the shaping of your body, the pacing, and rhythms that happen. Now, take a full in-breath and a long out-breath and return to the ice pack, the arm squeezes, the shaking, the patting of your chest to walk the resilience bridge. Oscillate between noticing shadow and connecting with your anchor. You may notice big emotions here, such as anger, sadness, grief, fear, and anxiety. Tell yourself, "It makes sense that this is coming up." Sequence the movements of these emotions with a good long out-breath and then return to stillness or a gentle repeating movement to ask yourself, "What is here now?" You may want to follow another movement or even go for a walk and then ask yourself again, "What is here now? What does my body want me to know?" Remind yourself that the structure of your body can hold you. Widen your somatic landscape with breath and panoramic awareness as you breathe into your back body and notice the shapes and colors in your periphery. Take time to thank your body for communicating with you and thank your partner for exploring this with you, for whatever amount of time and information you were able to surface.

The shadow is not a clear place to be, and it often takes several explorations to begin to form a clearer idea of what is ready to be worked with. This process of working with the shadow is not about processing and integrating everything. This is about practicing the ability to work with dysregulation, shadow, and trauma when it arises. As dance/movement therapist and human rights psychotherapist Amber Gray says:

> *"The past continues to influence us. It doesn't mean we will no longer be triggered or affected; it means we have restored our innate capacities to regulate, to ground, to remain centered and in ourselves in ways that don't undermine our living as they once did.*
>
> (Caldwell, 2024)

Make notes of what you notice and explore the following questions together:

- What are the statements (in your mind or to each other) that "hit play" when you are dysregulated? Where do these statements sound familiar from?
- What is your somatic experience here? Where might this feel familiar from?
- What beautiful and creative parts of you (golden shadow) are being suppressed here?
- Invite yourself to take a step back in your perspective—what is the overall shadow pattern that you see between you, and how do your shadows fit together like puzzle pieces? Make sure you are using the embodied communication language of, "I notice I feel *X* when you say *Y* or do *Z*," instead of saying, "You make me feel . . ."
- What autopilot activities do you turn to? What are the qualities of your autopilot, and what senses are being used (sight, taste, sound, touch, smell, kinesthetic)?
- What movements and activities engage your autopilot senses in a more active and nourishing way (resilience movements and activities)?

This process can bring up strong emotions, which can cause fatigue and greater sensitivity. Support each other to access resilience and engage in aftercare after exploring shadow. Aftercare and engaging resources begin to regulate your nervous system and get you grounded in your window of capacity so that you can integrate your new learning and reach a place of connection together, so don't skimp on this part. A good long rest and a strong dose of compassion is the right medicine.

Apply Erotic Mapping to Your Daily Life

Once you create your combined erotic map, take it with you (in your journal or in your mind) as you experience life together. When you are out on your favorite hike together (resource), share with each other what you are feeling in your inner somatic landscape. Notice the movement qualities that you express together and intentionally bring in the movement fundamentals—breathe deeper, volumize and extend your movements, take moments to yield, and breathe in the pleasure of the moment.

When you are experiencing challenge in the form of arousal non-concordance, anxiousness in initiating touch, or avoidance of some aspect of intimacy, ask yourself what your body needs to address the bound muscle tension, to soften the anxiousness, or to follow the inner impulse to lean toward your partner as you engage your resilience. Share with each other what you are experiencing and encourage each other to take your time here—let your partner know that you trust their body autonomy and that you are a team together. You won't get there faster by rushing. Instead, by slowing down in these moments and prioritizing intimacy, you are laying the groundwork for deeper and more lasting sexuality evolution.

AFTERWORD

Practice, Integrate, Transform

Your intimate relationship can be a vital source of co-created pleasure, personal meaningfulness, healing, and an expression of life force energy that changes with you throughout your life. Meaningful pleasure and connection volumize your genuine somatic expression to be more of who you genuinely are. You can weave bodyful moments of pleasure into your daily life by (1) supporting yourself and your partner to engage in daily personal pleasure practices and (2) prioritizing mutually pleasurable activities together.

A commitment to this practice is an investment in your overall quality of life as you deepen self-knowledge, personal empowerment, and physiological resilience, so you can weather the ups and downs of life with a deep well of resilient fire within. Your embodied intimacy with your partner is an opportunity to embrace this beautiful potential of being a human wired for pleasure and resilience.

Remember that your challenges are gateways to greater awareness and growth. Communication, emotional, and sexual challenges are not battles that you win—they are moments of important information—opportunities to know yourselves and each other better, to learn something new, to communicate relational boundaries, and to reaffirm what your connection means to you. Is your relationship growing with you? Are you discovering new things about yourself and your partner? Are you refining your approach to intimacy and playfulness? Keep your relationship awake and alive! When you approach relationships as a practice with evolutionary potential, you grow strength and tone in the nervous system to fully breathe into the shared moments. Actively and compassionately engage with the moments of flow and moments of challenge.

DOI: 10.4324/9781003508984-17

Your intimate relationship is a dance of nervous systems, personalities, and relational habits crafted over years of interactions with family, friends, other intimate partners, and some unwanted encounters, all within the impactful context of your culture, religion, socioeconomic position, and your natural and human-impacted environment. It is a rhythmic choreography that we engage in so that we can be seen and felt, to love and be loved. This is a dance that is compelling and fulfilling and also scary at times. It is the dance that you show up for with your full self, ready to amplify your gifts while inviting the best qualities of your partner to move with you.

Through intimate relationship, *you can feel yourselves.*

Take your time and slow your awareness with your partner as you continue to explore your shared moments. An embodied approach to relationship requires that you embrace nuance, widening your inner somatic landscape to embrace the complexity and ongoing learning that reveals layer after layer of your relationship, from your origin story to the present moment, to the future, and what you pass on through your lineage. Just as you benefited from whatever personal work your parents did, your children and your community will benefit from the personal work that you do. As you incorporate practices and intentionally shared values into your relationship, you are modeling for others what potential awaits them. This is how social change, like overlapping waves of growth and recession and continued growth, works on the larger social level. We all benefit from the personal growth that is done in each relationship, in each home.

The practices in this book are reliable tools for you to incorporate into your daily life to get more out of each moment of your precious time together. These daily practices give you the power to turn obstacles into doorways—to bridge back into your window of capacity from dysregulation, to explore safe-enough touch that can become an exhilarating gateway into arousal, and to transition into the realm of sexual response together as adventurers riding a wave at the pace of your connection.

Creation of new intimacy habits with each other goes beyond talking—this book has been an invitation to intentionally engage with bodyful practices in order to create new muscle memory and rhythms of relating. We don't improve any skill without focused practice. Diligence and repetition are the way as you start to invest your awareness in everyday eroticism.

I encourage you to choose one practice at a time to invest in together. Invest in a daily breath-supported hug, or a nightly bodyful touch practice, or weaving embodied consent into your "how was your day, honey" intentional transition check-in. Use the structured practices in this book and then let your personal style come through. Write your practice on paper and place it on your bathroom mirror or your fridge so that you are reminded of what you are practicing. Once you feel that you have integrated one practice, then add another, like studying your sexual response dynamic. Make it doable and make it interesting with no pressure to perform. If the performance instinct crops up, slow down and reconnect with what is true for you in the moment. Offer gratitude to each other and begin again.

Our world broadens when we love someone who loves something that is new to us. As you explore one practice at a time, remember that each of you brings something important to the dynamic. You get to learn so much about yourself, and you get to learn more about your partner. The somatic expression of your partner, the activities that they love, and their curiosities and priorities open you to a new dimension of life.

Take time to feel your partner's movements and excitement in your own body. Share your own movements and excitement with them. Inspire each other to feel seen and appreciated. Celebrate your autonomy and your togetherness. Savor those moments of attunement and flow.

This is when you get to say, "This is us. The essence of us." This embodied connection gives a sense of deeply felt purpose, a living mythology that will nourish your connection and remind you of who you truly are together through the triumphs and misadventures of your shared life.

REFERENCES

American Cancer Society, Shover. (n.d.). *Sex and the Adult Female with Cancer*. Retrieved from www.cancer.org

Amighi, J. K., Loman, S., & Sossin, M. (2018). *The Meaning of Movement* (2nd ed.). Routledge.

Atkinson, B. J. (2005). *Emotional Intelligence in Couples Therapy: Advances from Neurobiology and the Science of Intimate Relationships*. W.W. Norton & Company.

Atkinson, B. J. (n.d.) (Version 4.1). *Core Differences in Ways of Maintaining Emotional Stability: Developing Habits for Relationship Success*. Training material article.

Bainbridge Cohen, B. (2012). Sensing, Feeling and Action: The Experiential Anatomy of Body-Mind Centering® (3rd ed.). Wesleyan University Press.

Bankroft, J., & Jansen, E. (April, 2009). The dual control model: Current status and future directions. *The Journal of Sex Research*, 46(2–3), 121–42.

Basson, R. (2000). The female sexual response: A different model. *Journal of Sex & Marital Therapy*, 26, 51–65.

Bos, H., Shenkman G., & Stein, Y. (2021). The mediating role of attachment Avoidance in the association between sexual orientation and mental health. *Journal of Homosexuality*.

Burney-Scott, O. (March, 2025). Between First Blood and Lost Heat. Presentation, 2025 Virtual AASECT Institute.

Caldwell, C. (2018). *Bodyfulness: Somatic Practices for Presence, Empowerment, and Waking Up in this Life*. Shambhala Publications.

Caldwell, C. (2024). *Conscious Moving: An Embodied Guide for Healing, Learning, Contemplating, and Creating*. North Atlantic Books.

Cao, H., Zhou, N., Fine, M., Liang, Y., Li, J., & Mills-Koonce, W. R. (2017). Sexual minority stress and same-sex relationship well-being: A meta-analysis of research prior to the U.S. Nationwide legalization of same-sex marriage. *Journal of Marriage and Family*, 79(5), 1258–1277.

Corinna, H. (2021). *What Fresh Hell Is This? Perimenopause, Menopause, Other Indignities, and You*. Grand Central Publishing.

Csikszentmihalyi, M. (2009) *The Evolving Self: A Psychology for the Third Millennium*. Harper Collins.

Fern, J., Rickert, E., & Samaran, N. (2020). *Polysecure: Attachment, Trauma and Consensual Nonmonogamy*. Thorntree Press.

Frank, R. (2001). *Body of Awareness: A Somatic and Developmental Approach to Psychotherapy*, Cambridge, MA: Gestalt Press.

Gallese, V. (2004). Intentional Attunement. The Mirror Neuron System and Its Role in Interpersonal Relations. Interdisciplines. Org.

Gottman, J., & Silver, N. (2015). *The Seven Principles for Making Marriage Work: A Practical Guide from the Country's Foremost Relationship Expert*. Harmony.

Hackney, P. (2001). *Making Connections: Total Body Integration through Bartenieff Fundamentals*. Routledge.

Herman, J. L. (1992). *Trauma and Recovery*. Basic Books/Hachette Book Group.

Jackson, K. (May, 2022). Where contact improvisation meets dance/movement therapy: An embodied group artistic inquiry. *American Journal of Dance Therapy*, 44(1), 1–24.

Kaplan, H. (1995). *Sexual Desire Disorders: Dysfunctional Regulation of Sexual Motivation*. Routledge.

Kleinplatz, P. J., & Ménard, A. D. (2020). *Magnificent Sex: Lessons from Extraordinary Lovers*. Routledge.

Laban, R. (1966). *Choreutics*. Edited by Lisa Ulmann. London: Macdonald and Evans.

Levine, A., & Heller, R. (2010). *Attached: The New Science of Adult Attachment and How It Can Help You Find and Keep Love*. New York: Jeremy P. Tarcher/Penguin.

Martin, B. (2021). *The Art of Receiving and Giving: The Wheel of Consent*. Luminare Press.

Masters, W. H., & Johnson, V. E. (1966). *Human Sexual Response*. Little, Brown.

Mosconi, L. (2024). *The Menopause Brain: New Science Empowers Women to Navigate the Pivotal Transition with Knowledge and Confidence*. Penguin Random House.

Nagoski, E. (2015). *Come as You Are: The Surprising New Science That Will Transform Your Sex Life*. Simon & Schuster.

Pallaro, P. (Ed.). (1999). *Authentic Movement: Essays by Mary Starks Whitehouse, Janet Adler, and Joan Chodorow*. Jessica Kingsley Publishers.

Perel, E. (2007). *Mating in Captivity: Unlocking Erotic Intelligence*. HarperCollins.

Porges, S. (2011). *The Polyvagal Theory: Neurophysiological Foundations of Emotions, Attachment, Communication, Self-Regulation*. Norton & Co. Inc.

Roach, M. (2008). *Bonk: The Curious Coupling of Science and Sex*. W.W. Norton & Co.

Romm, A. (2021). *Hormone Intelligence: The Complete Guide to Calming Hormone Chaos and Restoring Your Body's Natural Blueprint for Well-Being*. HarperOne.

Safron, A. (Oct, 2016). What is orgasm? A model of sexual trance and climax via rhythmic entrainment. *Socioaffect Neurosci Psychol*, 6:31763. https://doi.org/10.3402/snp.v6.31763. PMID: 27799079; PMCID: PMC5087698.

Słowiński, P., Zhai, C., Alderisio, F., Salesse, R., Gueugnon, M., Marin, L., Bardy, B. G., di Bernardo, M., & Tsaneva-Atanasova, K. (March, 2016). Dynamic similarity promotes interpersonal coordination in joint action. *Journal of the Royal Society Interface*, 13(116), 20151093. https://doi.org/10.1098/rsif.2015.1093. PMID: 27009178; PMCID: PMC4843673.

Sutter, J. (2024). *The Sacred and the Sensual: A Multi-Dimensional Analysis of Evangelical Purity Culture's Influence on Women's Relationship with Their Body and Sexuality*. Retrieved from http://lup.lub.lu.se/student-papers/record/9156597

Sutton-Tyrrell, K., Selzer, F., Sowers, M. F. R., Finkelstein, J., Powell, L., Gold, E., Greendale, G., & Matthews, K. (2018). *Study of Women's Health Across the Nation (SWAN), 2006–2008: Visit 10 Dataset*. Inter-university Consortium for Political and Social Research [distributor], 2018-11-15. https://doi.org/10.3886/ICPSR32961.v2

Tanji, F., Kawajiri, M., Nanbu, H., & Nishimoto, D. (7 January, 2025). Uneven impact of andropause symptoms on daily life domains in employed men: A cross-sectional study. *Journal of Occupational Health*, 67(1), uiaf040. https://doi.org/10.1093/joccuh/uiaf040. PMID: 40643142; PMCID: PMC12341947

Tatkin, S. (2012). *Wired for Love: How Understanding Your Partner's Brain and Attachment Style Can Help You Defuse Conflict and Build a Secure Relationship*. New Harbinger Publications.

Winston, D. (2019). *The Little Book of Being: Practices and Guidance for Uncovering Your Natural Awareness*. Sounds True.

INDEX

Note: Page numbers in *italics* indicate a figure on the corresponding page.

www.ingramcontent.com/pod-product-compliance
Ingram Content Group UK Ltd.
Pitfield, Milton Keynes, MK11 3LW, UK
UKHW022018180926
475701UK00005B/904
* 9 7 8 1 0 3 2 8 3 2 5 1 7 *